Advanced Legal Research Exercise Manual

Kathleen A. Portuán Miller
Texas Tech University

WEST
THOMSON LEARNING

Australia Canada Mexico Singapore Spain United Kingdom United States

WEST
THOMSON LEARNING™

WEST LEGAL STUDIES

Advanced Legal Research Exercise Manual
by Kathleen A. Portuán Miller

Business Unit Director:
Susan L. Simpfenderfer

Executive Editor:
Marlene McHugh Pratt

Acquisitions Editor:
Joan M. Gill

Editorial Assistant:
Lisa Flatley

Executive Marketing Manager:
Donna J. Lewis

Channel Manager:
Nigar Hale

Executive Production Manager:
Wendy A. Troeger

Production Editor:
J.P. Henkel

Cover Design:
Dutton & Sherman

Cover Image:
Digital imagery® copyright 1999
PhotoDisc, Inc.

COPYRIGHT © 2001 Delmar
West Legal Studies is an imprint of Delmar,
a division of Thomson Learning, Inc. Thomson Learning™ is a trademark used herein under license

Printed in the (Country of printer)
2 3 4 5 XXX 05 04 02 01

For more information contact Delmar,
3 Columbia Circle, PO Box 15015,
Albany, NY 12212-5015.

Or find us on the World Wide Web at http://www.westlegalstudies.com

ALL RIGHTS RESERVED. No part of this work covered by the copyright hereon may be reproduced or used in any form or by any means—graphic, electronic, or mechanical, including photocopying, recording, taping, Web distribution or information storage and retrieval systems—without written permission of the publisher.

For permission to use material from this text or product, contact us by
Tel (800) 730-2214
Fax (800) 730-2215
www.thomsonrights.com

Library of Congress Cataloging-in-Publication Data
Miller, Kathleen A. Portuán.
Advanced legal research exercise manual
p.000 00.00cm.
Includes bibliographical references and index.
ISBN 0-7668-2024-6
1. Legal research—United States—Problems, exercises, etc.
2. Law—United States—Bibliography. I. Title

KF240 .M55 2000
340'.07'2073—dc21 00-043335

NOTICE TO THE READER

Publisher does not warrant or guarantee any of the products described herein or perform any independent analysis in connection with any of the product information contained herein. Publisher does not assume, and expressly disclaims, any obligation to obtain and include information other than that provided to it by the manufacturer.

The reader is notified that this text is an educational tool, not a practice book. Since the law is in constant change, no rule or statement of law in this book should be relied upon for any service to any client. The reader should always refer to standard legal sources for the current rule or law. If legal advice or other expert assistance is required, the services of the appropriate professional should be sought.

The Publisher makes no representation or warranties of any kind, including but not limited to, the warranties of fitness for particular purpose or merchantability, nor are any such representations implied with respect to the material set forth herein, and the publisher takes no responsibility with respect to such material. The publisher shall not be liable for any special, consequential, or exemplary damages resulting, in whole or part, from the readers' use of, or reliance upon, this material.

Acknowledgments

Thanks to the following people at Barry University of Orlando School of Law who helped me create this book:

Kathy Bowman, Administrative Assistant
Margaret Satterfield, Administrative Assistant
Mike Schau, Librarian
Warren McEwen, Librarian

Thanks also to the following reviewers:

Dora Dye, Freelance Paralegal
David M. Freeman, Community College of Philadelphia
Catherine McKee, St. San Antonio College
Eli Bortman, Suffolk University
Scott Rokely, Lansing Community College
Susan Harrell, University of West Florida
Clark Wheeler, Santa Fe Community College
Julie Murthy, Virginia Intermont College

and thanks to my parents Eva María and John

Table of Contents

Introduction

Today, lawyers and paralegals are doing more legal research on an advanced level than ever before. To be efficient at legal research, they need to have a solid understanding of how to use the law library (or other library) and legal computer. By developing the particular skills that legal researchers need through the use of exercises, law students and paralegals will become more proficient in finding solutions to research problems. Through these exercises, they will also become skilled at using the library and formulating research strategies.

SUBJECT AND APPROACH

Advanced Legal Research Exercise Manual is a practical text that covers legal research exercises on an advanced level, including legal exercises on business, bankruptcy, tax, patents and trademarks, employment and labor law, securities, international law, medical research, wills and estates, government documents and legislative history, environmental law, criminal law and procedure, Westlaw and Lexis problems, and Internet problems. The variety and number of exercise drills will enable students to have a well-rounded base for their overall research.

PURPOSE AND SCOPE

The book is designed as an exercise book for both law students and paralegals. The level is advanced research.

The book's unique features include

- chapter introductions with explanations of the subject area;
- new subject coverage of legal research areas such as bankruptcy, tax, business, medicine, Internet, and so on; and
- coverage at the advanced computer level.

CHAPTER 1

Business Resources

INTRODUCTION

Business entities in the United States are classified into three broad types: sole proprietorships, partnerships, and corporations.

A sole proprietorship is a business in which one person owns all the assets, owes all the liabilities, and operates in his or her own personal capacity.[1] Hence, a sole proprietor is merely a person in business for himself or herself and is, therefore, relatively free from legal encumbrances.

Partnerships are associations of two or more persons to carry on as co-owners of a business for profit.[2] A partnership may be a formal, written agreement or a simple verbal one. Both are legally enforceable. Moreover, people not even intending a partnership may be held to have created a partnership, called partnership by estoppel.[3] The dissolution of a partnership occurs when the partners cease to carry on the business of the partnership together.[4]

Partnerships are further categorized as general or limited.[5] In a general partnership, all partners have the same power and accountability as to duties and obligations, whether they participate in the operation of the business or not. In a limited partnership, at least one general partner has the same obligations and responsibilities of a partner in a general partnership, but at least one limited partner does not participate in the operation of the business and has liability limited to the amount of capital contributed.[6]

Unlike a corporation, a partnership is usually not considered a separate legal entity distinct from its principles. Originally, partnerships had their foundation in the common law. In the early twentieth century, the Uniform Partnership Act (UPA) and the Uniform Limited Partnership Act (ULPA) were promulgated to standardize the rules governing partnerships and limited partnerships. These acts codified the existing partnership laws.[7] The UPA was published in 1914 by the National Conference of Commissioners on Uniform State Laws, an organization founded in 1892 and dedicated to the concept of uniform laws. The UPA has been adopted in forty-nine states and in several territories as well.[8] Although the UPA was revised in 1994, the revised act, RUPA, has been substituted for the original act in only a few states. The UPA has more than forty sections and contains rules for partnership existence, the relationship of the partners, and relationship of the partnership to outside parties. Also detailed is the process of dissolution of the partnership.[9] The Uniform Limited Partnership Act (ULPA), published in 1916, was also a product of the National Conference of Commissioners on Uniform State Laws. A 1976 revision of the ULPA loosened the stranglehold on the activities of the limited partner. A limited partner may now contribute services to the partnership, although his/her participation in the control and management of the partnership is still restricted. Additionally, a limited partner may be granted voting rights and is ensured of the right to inspect the partnership records.[10] The partnership remains a nebulous entity, distinguished from its partners but not an "artificial person" on its own. It is important to refer to the Uniform Partnership Act and the Uniform Limited Partnership Act to ascertain the rights, duties, and obligations of the individual partners as well the partnership itself.

A corporation is an "artificial person" created by authority of statute. A foreign corporation refers to any corporation organized under the laws of another forum, either another state or another country.[11] Corporations are classified into several different types depending on a variety of factors. These types include whether the partnership is public, private for profit, or charitable not-for-profit.[12] Additionally, corporations are classified according to the number of investors, one or more, and as to whether the stock is publicly traded.[13]

A corporation receives its charter—permission to operate—from its forum state.[14] A corporation's board of directors runs the business according to its charter and bylaws.[15] Corporations raise capital to operate by issuing securities, stocks, and bonds, which are sold to investors. Investors who are shareholders are usually entitled to vote for the corporation's board of directors.[16] Unlike a partnership, a corporation is a separate legal entity, and its principles, employees, shareholders, and investors are not personally liable for the debts of the corporation.[17] When researching a corporate legal issue, it is important to consider all the possible laws that affect the corporation. These laws include the statutory law of the forum state, the administrative laws of the Internal Revenue Service, and the Securities and Exchange Commission.

HINTS

Most of the companies in the United States have their own Internet addresses. For example, H.J. Heinz has http://www.Heinz.com.

GETTING STARTED

A good way to begin research of a company for basic business information is by checking in a directory such as the *Million Dollar Directory; Standard and Poor's Register of Corporations, Directors and Executives*; or *Thomas Register of American Manufacturers*. For financial information about the companies, see *Moody's Complete Corporate Index* and *Value Line Investment Survey*. Annual reports, 10K reports, and 10Q reports are available in hard copy at public libraries and also on Westlaw (SEC-10K and SEC 10Q) and Lexis (COMPNY;10K, or COMPNY;10Q, or COMPNY;ARS). The New York Stock Exchange is available on the Internet at http: / /www.NYSE.com.

BIBLIOGRAPHY

Statistical Sources

U.S. Bureau of the Census. *Statistical Abstract of the United States*. Washington, D.C.: U.S. Government Printing Office (annual). This publication is probably the most important U.S. statistical reference work because it serves both as a prime source for U.S. industrial, social, political, and economic statistics and as a bibliographic guide. HA202.

U.S. Bureau of Labor Statistics. *Monthly Labor Review*. Washington, D.C.: U.S. Government Printing Office (monthly). This publication provides current labor statistics covering employment, unemployment, hours, consumer and product indexes, wages and compensation, and work stoppages. HD8051 .A78.

Dictionaries

Jay M. Shafritz and Daniel Oran. *The New American Dictionary of Business & Finance*. New York: Penguin Group, 1990. HF 1001 .S3 1990.

Directories

Encyclopedia of Associations. Detroit, Mich.: Gale Research Company, 1999. This book is a comprehensive listing of all types of national organizations in the United States. For each association, this directory provides the name of the chief officer, a brief statement of activities, the number of members, publications, dates of meetings, and so on. HF1001 .S3 A522 .E5.

Million Dollar Directory. Parsippany, N.J.: Dun's Marketing Services (annual). This four-volume set contains approximately 115,000 U.S. businesses with an indicated worth of over $500,000. For each business, it gives officers and directors, line of business, Standard Industrial Classification (SIC) code, approximate sales, number of employees, and so on. Each volume contains a geographic index and an index by SIC industry; there is also a master index for the four volumes. HC 102 .D8 1999.

Standard & Poor's Register of Corporations, Directors and Executives. New York: Standard & Poor's Corporation (annual). This directory has three volumes (with 3 cumulative supplements); it is a major reference source that covers both U.S. and large Canadian companies and contains a list of the companies, executives and directors, and so on, and a complete index. HG 4057 .A4. 1999.

Thomas Register of American Manufacturers and *Thomas Register Catalog File*. New York: Thomas Publishing Company, 17 volumes (annual). This is the best place to find the name of a U.S. manufacturing firm or to find who makes a specific product. Volumes 1–9 list over 115,000 U.S. manufacturers by specific product or service; volumes 10–11 contain the list of catalogs arranged alphabetically, and volumes 12–17 are catalogs of companies. T12 .T6. 1999.

Local Directories

Dun's Regional Business Directory. New Jersey: Dun & Bradstreet Information Services (annual). This directory contains information on sales, president, and so on.

Services

Moody's Complete Corporate Index. New York: Moody's Investors' Service, 1999. (Seven Moody's financial manuals make up this set; 3 issues per year). Six of these manuals contain important financial information about companies listed on the U.S. exchanges; the international manual covers leading foreign companies. The statistical data varies with each type of manual. *Moody's Complete Index* makes it easy to determine in which of these manuals one can find any individual company. HG 4961 .M66 1999.

Value Line Investment Survey. New York: A. Bernhard & Company, 1999 (loose-leaf with weekly additions). This popular investment service continuously analyzes and reports on 1,700 companies in about 95 industries. The statistics, charts, and brief explanatory text are reviewed and updated—industry by industry—on a rotating basis so that the information on each company in every industry is revised quarterly. HG 4501 .V24 1999.

Annual reports, 10K reports, and 10Q reports. These reports are available at your local public library, business library, or university library (general collection); on the Internet; or on Lexis and Westlaw.

An annual report is a company's financial statement prepared yearly for stockholders; it is available upon request for those other than stockholders. It gives comparative financial statements for the current and past years. Some annual reports give divisional reports of past activities and future plans.

A 10K is the annual report required by the SEC of publicly held corporations that sell stock. It must be submitted within 3 months after the close of its fiscal year. It includes a set of financial statements, a description of the company's business, a list of the securities and properties owned by the company, a summary of the last 5 years of operation, and an analysis of financial reports.

A 10Q is a condensed form of the 10K, which a public company must file with the SEC within 45 days of the end of each reporting quarter.

Computer Sources

Westlaw

DUNBR (Dun & Bradstreet, Business Records, extra fee)
S&PCorp. (Standard & Poor's, extra fee)
TRO (Thomas Register)
SECNOW (electronic filings of the SEC)
EDGAR
SEC-10Q
SEC-10K

Lexis

BUSFIN;ABI (articles/journals—business)
COMPNY;INVTXT (Moody's)
COMPNY;FILING (SEC and EDGAR filings)
COMPNY;ACCESS (comprehensive listing of SEC filings of a particular company)
COMPNY;10Q
COMPNY;10K
COMPNY;ARS
COMPNY;SPCORP (executives company information)

Internet Resources

http://cnn.com
http://www.NYSE.com

ENDNOTES

1. *Black's Law Dictionary*, 7th ed. (St. Paul, Minn.: West, 1999), 1398.
2. Martin Weinstein, *Summary of American Law* (Rochester, N.Y.: The Lawyers' Cooperative Publishing Company, 1988).
3. Ibid., 53.
4. Ibid., 55.
5. Ibid., 50.
6. Ibid., 51.
7. Ibid., 49.
8. Daniel S. Kleinberger, *Agency and Partnership* (1995), 199.
9. Ibid., 199, 200.
10. National Conference of Commissioners, Revised Uniform Limited Partnership Act, Dec. 27, 1997. Available: http://www.nccusl.org/summary/ulpa.html
11. Weinstein, 56.
12. Ibid., 57.
13. Ibid., 56.
14. Ibid., 59.
15. Ibid., 63.
16. Ibid., 60.
17. Ibid., 62.

ASSIGNMENT A

Business Research

Sources

Dollar Million Directory
Moody's Complete Corporate Index
Standard and Poor's Register of Corporations, Directors and Executives
Thomas Register of American Manufacturers and Thomas Register Catalog File
The Value Line Investment Survey
ABI Inform, General Business File, Newspaper Abstracts, Uncover, Business Newsbank (free at your local public library)
Lexis (NEWS;ALLNEWS or BUSFIN;ABI) and Westlaw (JLR or ABI-INFORM)
Internet (search for the particular company)

1. Your law firm has received a call from XYZ Corporation. XYZ wants to meet to discuss some potential litigation involving a sexual harassment suit. The senior partner has asked you to find answers to the following questions:

   a. What are the corporation's address, telephone, founding date, CEO and president, bank, state of incorporation, amount of sales, and number of employees? (Hint: Try the *Million Dollar Directory* or *Standard & Poor's*.)

   b. What are the corporation's assets?

   c. Who are the managers of the company?

   d. Is the company involved in other litigation? (Hint: Search on Westlaw: ti(Heinz); or Lexis: name(Heinz.)

   e. Does it have in-house counsel? (Hint: Search on Lexis or Westlaw under Heinz.)

   f. What are the company's total revenues and share earnings? (Hint: Check *Value Line*.)

   g. Find a relevant new article about the company.

   Pick your own company and research the answers to the above questions. Show your search strategy.

ASSIGNMENT B

Business Resources

Sources

CNN Website: http://cnn.com
H.J. Heinz Company Website: http://www.Heinz.com
New York Stock Exchange Website: http://www.NYSE.com

For this assignment, you need to find some background material on the H.J. Heinz Company using the Internet. You will find that Heinz has its own Website (http://www.Heinz.com), just as many companies do.

When you are in the Heinz Website, go into "Showcase Brands."

1. What was the first Heinz product? How was it packed? Why?

2. As one of Heinz's holdings, what is the largest weight loss program in the United States and how many members does it have?

3. Who is the world's leading tuna processor, which is another of Heinz's holdings?

4. What dog food is under Heinz's auspices?

5. What is Spain's equivalent of Heinz ketchup?

6. What type of business does Heinz have in Zimbabwe? What are its products?

7. Go into "Investor Relations" in the Heinz Website. What percentage of retail sales in the United States does Heinz have?

8. Go to the New York Stock Exchange Website (http://www.NYSE.com) and search "H J Heinz." What is the last trade price per share for Heinz stock?

9. Is the price per share up or down?

10. Find a story dated June 15, 1999, about H.J. Heinz. Did the company report an increase or a decrease for the fourth quarter?

11. Who is the president and CEO?

12. Click on "Global Investing; International View." Then search "Heinz and Japan." What type of business is Heinz doing in Japan?

13. Go into CNN's Website (http://www.cnn.com) and search "Heinz." Find a story on "The World's Billionaires According to Forbes Magazine" (June 20,1999). Locate the former president and CEO of Heinz, Irishman, Anthony J. O'Reilly. What is his net worth?

CHAPTER 2

Bankruptcy

INTRODUCTION

Historians have traced the origins of bankruptcy law to Roman law in 118 B.C. Centuries later, when the U.S. Constitution was framed in 1787, Congress was given the right to establish "uniform laws of bankruptcy."[1] The first American bankruptcy law of 1800 copied similar English laws. This law was superseded by the Bankruptcy Act of 1898, which remained in effect until 1979. A common characteristic of bankruptcy statutes is that all the creditors are compelled to accept some arrangement or some disposition of their claims against the bankrupt's property.

Bankruptcy laws provide a means of sorting the rights of claimants against the available assets. The distribution of assets among creditors is the center of the bankruptcy scheme. Whereas state and federal nonbankruptcy laws provide a means to collect a single debt, bankruptcy law is a collective debt-collection system, which also can provide a fresh start for certain debtors.

Bankruptcy law is federal law, and it is primarily statutory law. It is title 11 of the U.S. Code. Bankruptcy cases filed prior to October 1, 1979, are governed by the Act of 1898, whereas cases filed after October 1, 1979, are governed by the Bankruptcy Reform Act of 1978, commonly referred to as the Bankruptcy Code.

The legislative history of the Bankruptcy Code is massive—it begins in 1968 and ends with the enactment of the Code in 1978. The Bankruptcy Code was amended in 1984, 1986, 1988, and 1990, and became the Bankruptcy Rules. These rules govern procedures in the United States Bankruptcy Courts.

Bankruptcy law also includes state law. There are basic differences between bankruptcy law and state law. First, state law puts a premium on prompt action—the first filing gets first preference. Second, the prospects for debtor relief are greater in state bankruptcy courts, and the prospects for a fresh start are better. Third, the vocabulary of bankruptcy law is different from that of state law—therefore, it is important to check the definition of statutory terms.

Some vocabulary words used in a bankruptcy case are:

1. Nobody is a bankrupt.
2. A debtor is the person being acted against.
3. A holder of a claim is a creditor.
4. A holder of a secured claim is a creditor with a lien on property of the debtor.
5. A holder of an unsecured claim is a creditor who does not have a lien on a debtor's property, or who has a lien on property of a lesser value than the claim.

6. The bankruptcy judge is a judicial officer of the district court.
7. The trustee is a representative of the creditors, generally appointed by the U.S. trustee.
8. A U.S. trustee is a federal government official who performs appointing and administrative tasks.
9. A creditor's committee is composed of representatives of creditors in Chapter 11 cases.
10. A debtor in possession is the debtor in a Chapter 11 or a Chapter 12 case.
11. An examiner is appointed in some Chapter 11 cases to investigate and perform such duties as the court might order.

There are two general forms of bankruptcy: liquidation and rehabilitation. Chapter 7 of the Bankruptcy Code is liquidation, where the trustees collect and distribute the assets of the debtor. Chapters 11, 12, and 13 of the Bankruptcy Code contemplate debtor rehabilitation.

A Chapter 7 case has five stages:

1. The debtor files the petition with the Bankruptcy Court.
2. The bankruptcy trustee collects the property of the estate of the debtor.
3. The trustee converts the collected property to cash (called liquidation).
4. The trustee distributes the results of the liquidation phase to holders of unsecured claims (called distribution).
5. The debtor is released from any further liability (called a discharge).

In a Chapter 13 case, the debtor retains title to his/her property and proposes a plan to pay creditors. Only individual debtors with regular income can file a Chapter 13 case. A Chapter 13 case has three stages:

1. The individual debtor files a petition.
2. Creditors are paid from the debtor's postpetition earnings.
3. The debtor is discharged when he/she finishes making the scheduled payments.

A Chapter 11 case usually involves business cases and rehabilitation. It will have the following stages:

1. Getting the debtor into bankruptcy.
2. Operating a business.
3. Making a plan of rehabilitation.
4. Getting creditor acceptance.
5. Receiving court confirmation.
6. Getting a discharge as a result of confirmation.
7. Making payments under the plan.

The differences between Chapter 7 and Chapter 11 are:

1. Every Chapter 7 case has a trustee.
2. In a Chapter 7 case, the trustee takes possession of the property and liquidates it; whereas in a Chapter 11 case, the debtor retains the property.

3. In a Chapter 11 case, the debtor receives a discharge when his/her plan is confirmed; whereas in a Chapter 7 case, discharge depends on the creditor's approval.

The differences between Chapter 11 and Chapter 13 cases are:

1. Debtors and creditors can file a Chapter 11 petition; only debtors can file Chapter 13 petitions.
2. Chapter 13 is restricted to individuals with regular income.
3. Chapter 11 contemplates creditor and debtor future plans; Chapter 13 does not.
4. In Chapter 11, creditors vote on the plan.
5. In Chapter 13 cases, discharge depends on debtor performance; in Chapter 11, discharge occurs when the plan is confirmed.

Chapter 12 was added to the Bankruptcy Code effective November 9, 1986. It gives alternative bankruptcy for the family farmer and is modeled on, and similar to, a Chapter 13 case.

HINTS

The prescription for finding bankruptcy material is to use a good loose-leaf service, such as Commerce Clearing House's *Bankruptcy Law Reporter*, which includes laws, court decisions, and rules of court; it also tracks federal legislation.

BIBLIOGRAPHY

Code

Bankruptcy Code, Collier Bankruptcy Edition. New York: Lawrence Piking, 1998. KF 1524 .C59 1954.

Treatises

Collier on Bankruptcy. New York: Matthew Bender, 1999. This publication is a comprehensive source of bankruptcy law information. It is written to meet the needs of bankruptcy practitioners and focuses on the current state of the law with the coverage of historical developments and expert opinions on unclear issues. In addition to forms, relevant legislation and court opinions are included. KF 1524 .C6 1940.

Bankruptcy Law Reporter. Chicago: Commerce Clearing House, 1999. This publication provides complete and timely coverage of federal bankruptcy, reorganization, and debt-restructuring laws under the Bankruptcy Code Act. It also includes rules and court decisions affecting bankruptcy law and digests that have exemption statutes. In addition, it tracks federal legislation and Supreme Court docket. KF 1520 .C65 1952.

Norton Bankruptcy Law and Practice. St. Paul, Minn.: West, 1999. This publication is a comprehensive survey of all aspects of bankruptcy law and procedure, from the initial client interview forward. A 12-volume treatise, the publication includes court organization and powers; administrative powers; claims and distributions to creditors; debtor duties and benefits; stockholder liquidations; tax consequences; Chapter 7 (liquidation); Chapters 9, 11, 12, and 13 litigation aspects of bankruptcy; interrelations of bankruptcy with related laws; and statutory tables. KF 1524 .N67.

Forms

Herzog's Bankruptcy Forms and Practice. Chicago: Commerce Clearing House, 1999. This publication provides the most complete collection of bankruptcy forms available—written, revised, and reviewed by experts in the field. It contains forms, practice notes, and comments to help complete the forms. There are also new and revised forms that reflect the revisions that the Advisory Committee has made in the Bankruptcy Rules and analyzes the impact of recent developments in the Rules and Code. KF 1527 .H45 1975

Newsletters

Norton Bankruptcy Law Advisor. Chicago: Commerce Clearing House, 1999. This newsletter focuses on the developments and trends that affect bankruptcy attorneys every day: Chapter 11 cases, Chapter 13 cases, the impact of Code §1111(b) on financial obligations of nondebtor partners, U.S. Trustee Programs BGOA conclusions, the new value exception, public pension benefits, and retirement plans. KF 1507 .N67.

Digests

West's Bankruptcy Digest. St. Paul, Minn.: West, 1999. This digest indexes state and federal cases under the topic of bankruptcy. It provides a cumulative index to the reported decisions of the U.S. Bankruptcy Courts, plus the bankruptcy decisions of the U.S. District Courts, U.S. Courts of Appeals, and the U.S. Supreme Court. It also includes bankruptcy points of laws from state courts. The publication uses West's key numbers; it has a Table of Cases, Descriptive Word Index, Table of Statutes, Bankruptcy Rules, and forms. KF 1515.3 .W48 1988.

Hornbooks

David G. Epstein, Steve H. Nickles, and James J. White. *Bankruptcy*. 1st ed. St. Paul, Minn.: West, 1993.

Nutshells

David G. Epstein, *Bankruptcy and Other Debtor—Creditor Law in a Nutshell*. 5th ed. St. Paul, Minn.: West, 1995.

Computer Sources

Westlaw

FBKR-All
FBKR-CS (Cases)
FBKR-USCA
FBKR-Rules

Lexis

MEGA;BANKR
BKRTCY;CASES
BKRTCY;BKRULE (Rules & Forms)
FORMS;LLFORM (Legal Forms)

Internet Sites

Chapter 7 Bankruptcy: http://www.chapter7.com

ENDNOTES

1. This section is based on David G. Epstein, *Bankruptcy* (St. Paul, Minn.: West, 1992).

ASSIGNMENT A

Bankruptcy

A good source for finding solutions to bankruptcy problems is to use loose-leaf services. Some widely used loose-leaf services include those by Commerce Clearing House (CCH), Collier, or Callaghan. Loose-leaf services are good in the bankruptcy area because (1) relevant law is collected in one place; that is, statutes, rules, and regulations and secondary materials are all in one place; (2) access is very current; (3) there is speed in publication and updating; (4) there is integrated coverage; that is, loose-leaf services cut across jurisdictional lines.

Sources

Collier on Bankruptcy
CCH Bankruptcy Law Reporter
Herzog's Bankruptcy Forms and Practice
Norton Bankruptcy Law Advisor
Note: Use the *Blue Book: Uniform System of Citation* to cite your sources.

1. Find *Collier on Bankruptcy* and locate the section on discharge that leads you to the *Smiley v. First National Bank of Belleville*. Cite to *Smiley*.

2. Find the CCH *Bankruptcy Law Reporter* and look in the topical index. Locate the paragraph number (¶) under "Accounts Receivable, Payment Under Factoring Agreements." Cite the *Toderelli* case and your loose-leaf source.

3. Use Herzog's *Bankruptcy Forms and Practice*, and, by using the index in volume 2, copy the form on Meeting of Creditors and Fixing Dates B Notice of Commencement of Corporation or Partnership Chapter 11 Case.

4. Find the *Norton Bankruptcy Law Advisor* published by Callaghan & Company and cite the article about the Constitutional Wall for Bankruptcy by C. Cohen in the June issue.

ASSIGNMENT B

Bankruptcy

Olga Opal had a very expensive opal, diamond, and ruby necklace, which was a family heirloom. Six months before she filed for bankruptcy, Olga obtained a loan from the Unlimited Loan Company and gave Unlimited a valid security interest in the necklace to secure the loan. The proceeds of the loan were used to pay off a number of credit card debts. At the time of bankruptcy, the balance of the loan was $5,000. The necklace was valued at $6,000. Opal wants to cash in the ring. What are the requirements of sections 722 and 522 of the Bankruptcy Code? Explain in detail; discuss whether the equity is exemptable and whether an individual debtor may redeem tangible personal property from a lien. Cite an appropriate case.

Sources

Bankruptcy Code (Collier Pamphlet Edition)

ASSIGNMENT C

Bankruptcy

Sources

Norton Bankruptcy Law and Practice
David G. Epstein, *Bankruptcy*
West's *Bankruptcy Digest*
Collier Bankruptcy Guide
Lexis
Westlaw

1. Use *Norton Bankruptcy Law and Practice* (1999) to find a form for relief under Chapter 11.

2. Locate a hornbook on bankruptcy and explain the "Wild Card" Exemption. (Hint: Use a hornbook: David Epstein's *Bankruptcy*.)

3. Locate West's *Bankruptcy Digest*. Use the Descriptive Word Index to find out which persons are entitled to file claims, particularly concerning labor unions in the Southern District of New York. Look up and cite the 1989 case. You can also search on Lexis (MEGA;BANKR) or Westlaw (FBKR-ALL). Who filed for reorganization under Chapter 11? What did the claim allege and seek?

4. Find the Omnibus Budget Reconciliation Act of 1993 and locate the checklist for Real Estate debt. (Hint: Use the *Collier Bankruptcy Practice Guide.*)

CHAPTER 3

Tax Research

INTRODUCTION

The theory underlying taxation is that charges are imposed to support the government in exchange for the general advantages and protection afforded by the government to the taxpayer and his or her property.[1] Government is a necessity that cannot continue without financial means to pay its expenses; therefore, the government has the right to compel all citizens and property within its limits to share its costs. Even ancient governments levied taxes. During the Roman Empire, especially during periods of high inflation, the government often collected taxes in kind, or goods, rather than in money. However, sometimes the Roman government was thwarted in its efforts to maintain extensive tax records, because angry taxpayers burned records during revolts.

The Sixteenth Amendment to the U.S. Constitution states, "The Congress shall have the power to lay and collect taxes on income from whatever sources derived, without apportionment among the several States, and without regard to any census or enumeration." This amendment was proposed by Congress on July 12, 1909, and ratified on February 3, 1913, when the amendment was approved.

Following the Sixteenth Amendment came the Revenue Act of 1913, also known as the Tariff Act of 1913. Thus, a series of revenue acts, which were passed every 2 or 3 years, came forth. Each act superseded each predecessor, reenacting provisions still in effect and amending provisions as needed.

On February 10, 1939, Congress passed the Internal Revenue Code of 1939. Prior to this Code, only revenue acts existed. This codification of tax laws contained the statutes of the United States (relating exclusively to revenue) that were in force as of January 2, 1939. The Internal Revenue Code (IRC) of 1939 was published as a separate volume of the Statutes at Large in 53 Stat. 1.

From 1939 to 1954, tax legislation was passed as amendments to the 1939 Code. The Internal Revenue Code of 1954, 68 Stat. 1, was a comprehensive revision of the revenue laws. The IRC was the result of over 2 years of work by the House Ways and Means Committee. Unlike the 1939 Code, which simply codified and reissued the revenue law then in effect, the IRC of 1954 included a "management of the provisions to place revenue laws in a more logical sequence, the deletion of obsolete material, and an attempt to express the Internal Revenue laws in a more understandable manner." In addition to the cosmetic changes, Congress made substantive changes in the law to "remove inequities, to end harassment of the taxpayer, and to reduce tax barriers to future expansion of production and employment."

The Internal Revenue Code of 1954 constituted Title 26 of the U.S. Code until 1986. All tax legislation enacted from 1954 to 1986 was passed as amendments to the 1954 IRC.

HINTS

1. A good hornbook provides a wealth of information in the tax area.
2. The Internal Revenue Hotline has experts that can answer just about any question. Call the Taxpayer Advocate at 800-829-1040 or 800-829-0433.

BIBLIOGRAPHY

Loose-Leaf Services

CCH Federal Estate and Gift Tax Reporter. Chicago, Ill.: Commerce Clearing House, 1999. This publication provides an in-depth analysis related to federal estate, gift, and generation-skipping tax law. It is essential for planning federal transfer tax consequences; it is Code based and integrates the text of the Code, regulations, and court decisions with CCH's explanations and other related authoritative documents. KF 6571 .A8 .C65.

CCH Standard Federal Tax Reporter. Chicago, Ill.: Commerce Clearing House, 1999. This publication has been the cornerstone of federal income tax research since 1913. This 22-volume loose-leaf publication provides a complete and up-to-date picture of federal income law, federal laws, regulations, administrative materials, and agency decisions in taxation. The publication is organized by Internal Revenue Code for quick and easy research. KF 6285 .C67.

CCH Federal Tax Service. Chicago, Ill.: Commerce Clearing House, 1999. This publication is a detailed and topically arranged analysis written by expert tax practitioners on how the federal tax law has been applied to specific real-world situations. This loose-leaf has numerous practical examples and sample calculations. KF 6285.C22.

RIA Federal Tax Coordinator. New York: Research Institute of America, 1999. This 35-volume loose-leaf publication provides in-depth analysis of federal tax questions as they arise in practice. Coverage includes FICA, FUTA, estate, gift, and excise taxes. The Coordinator provides observations, cautions, illustrations, and recommendations by professional tax editors. HJ 3252 .F4.

U.S. Tax Reporter. New York: Research Institute of America, 1999. This loose-leaf deals with income tax law, legislation, and regulations. It is kept up to date by weekly bulletins. KF 6285 .P734.

Cases/Decisions/Rulings

CCH Tax Court Memorandum Decisions. Chicago, Ill.: Commerce Clearing House, 1999. This publication contains a court's decision that gives the ruling (what the court decides and orders done) but not the opinion (reason for the decision). KF 6324 .A51 .C6.

U.S. Tax Cases Reporter. Chicago, Ill.: Commerce Clearing House, 1999. This publication contains U.S. tax cases from the U.S. Supreme Court, U.S. Circuit Courts, U.S. District Courts, U.S. Federal Court of Federal Claims, and U.S. Bankruptcy Court. KF 6324 .A7 .C6.

IRS Letter Rulings. Chicago, Ill.: Commerce Clearing House, 1999. These are written statements issued to a taxpayer by the Office of the Assistant Commissioner of the IRS in which interpretations of tax laws are made and applied to a specific set of facts. KF 6289 .A353.

Codes

Internal Revenue Code. St. Paul, Minn.: West, 1995. This publication contains the full text of the current Internal Revenue Code, including CCH's comprehensive Code-amendment notes to allow tracking of changes over time. KF 6276 .S26 .A19 .I57.

Government Publications

IRS Cumulative Bulletin. Washington, D.C.: U.S. Government Printing Office, 1999. This bulletin contains Revenue Rulings, which express an official interpretation of the tax laws as applied to specific transactions.

Treasury Decisions. Washington, D.C.: U.S. Government Printing Office, 1999. This publication includes rulings, court decisions, or regulations.

Hornbooks

Michael D. Rose and John C. Crommie. *Federal Income Taxation.* 3rd ed. St. Paul, Minn.: West, 1988 with 1994–95 pocket part. KF 6369 .R67 1988.

Nutshells

John J. McNulty. *Federal Estate and Gift Taxation in a Nutshell.* 5th ed. St. Paul, Minn.: West, 1994. KF 6572 .Z9 .M3 1994.

John J. McNulty. *Federal Income Taxation of Individuals in a Nutshell.* 5th ed. St. Paul, Minn.: West, 1995. KF 6369.3 .M3 1995.

Patricia T. Morgan. *Tax Procedure and Tax Fraud in a Nutshell.* 2nd ed. St. Paul, Minn.: West, 1999. KF 6324 .Z9 .M67 1999.

Computer Sources

Westlaw

FTX-CS (Federal Case Law)
FTX-USCA (U.S. Code Annotated)
FTX-TXT
FTX-CB (Cumulative Bulletin)

Lexis

FEDTAX;Cases
FEDTAX;USCS (Tax Court)
FEDTAX;TCM (Tax Court Memo)
FEDTAX;CB

Internet Sites

SBTtek Law and Tax Website Directory (or the Digital Diary—IRS) is the Internal Revenue Service's home page on the World Wide Web. The goal of this Website is to provide immediate access to IRS tax information and services: http://www.sbt.net/law.html.

ENDNOTES

1. This section is based on *The Guide to American Law: Everyone's Legal Encyclopedia* (St. Paul, Minn.: West, 1984), 3.1.

ASSIGNMENT A

Tax Research

Sources

CCH Standard Federal Tax Reporter
U.S. Tax Reporter
Revenue Rulings (in the IRS Cumulative Bulletin)
Lexis
Westlaw

1. Your client owns a small grocery store, which is housed in the same building in which he lives. He wants to trade this building for a home in the suburbs to avoid capital gains taxes. Both properties are of roughly equal value. Will this transaction qualify for capital gains as a like-kind exchange? Use both the *CCH Standard Federal Tax Reporter* and Research Institute of America's *U.S. Tax Reporter* to compare and contrast your answer. (Hint: Try subject headings such as Non-Recognition of Gain or Loss from Exchanges Solely in Kind.)

   Cite your sources according to the Bluebook.

2. Look in the *IRS Cumulative Bulletin* on 1997-1, January–June, by the Department of the Treasury, and find Revenue Ruling 97-21. What issue does this Revenue Ruling deal with? What was the holding of the Internal Revenue Service?

ASSIGNMENT B

Tax Research

Sources

U.S. Tax Cases (CCH)
U.S. Tax Reporter: Estate and Gift Taxes
Tax Court Memorandum Decisions
Westlaw
Lexis

1. Using *U.S. Tax Cases* by CCH, volume 95-1, find a case concerning bad debts and deductibility/valuation and cite the case.

2. Find the *U.S. Tax Reporter: Estate and Gift Taxes* by Research Institute of America (RIA) and locate the section about stock options and marital deductions. Cite the *Critchfield* case. What is the Internal Revenue Code under which this case falls?

3. Use Westlaw or Lexis and check the status of any bills dealing with federal excise taxes. For Lexis, use FEDTAX/LEGIS; on Westlaw, use BNA-TRACK. Limit your search to June 1994. Show your search strategy and name three items that are subject to federal excise taxes.

4. Find TC Memorandum Decisions 1994, vol. 1 &94,407 TC Memo 2994-407 Humberto OROZCO and Helena OROZCO, Docket 16207-92. Were the taxpayers entitled to depreciation for an immigrant documentation computer program? Why or why not?

CHAPTER 4

Patent, Trademark, and Copyright Law

INTRODUCTION

Some people confuse patents, trademarks, and copyrights. Although these intellectual property protections do have some similarities, they are different and serve different purposes.[1]

A patent for an invention is the grant of a property right to the inventor, issued by the Patent and Trademark Office. The term of a new patent is 20 years from the date on which the application for the patent was filed in the United States. U.S. patent grants are effective only within the United States, U.S. territories, and U.S. possessions.

The right conferred by the patent grant is, in the language of the patent act statute, 35 U.S.C. §101 et seq. (1999) and of the grant itself, "the right to exclude others from asking, using, offering for sale, or selling the invention in the United States or importing the invention into the United States." What is granted is not the right to make, use, offer for sale, sell, or import, but the right to exclude others from making, using, offering for sale, selling, or importing the invention.

A trademark is a word, name, symbol, or device that is used in trade with goods to indicate the source of the goods of others. A servicemark is the same as a trademark except that it identifies and distinguishes the source of a service rather than a product. The terms *trademark* and *mark* are commonly used to refer to both trademarks and servicemarks.

Trademark rights may be used to prevent others from using a confusingly similar mark, but not to prevent others from making the same goods or from selling the same goods or services under a clearly different mark. Trademarks used in interstate or foreign commerce may be registered with the Patent and Trademark Office.

A copyright is a form of protection provided to the authors of original works, including literary, dramatic, musical, artistic, and certain other intellectual works, both published and unpublished. The 1976 Copyright Act generally gives the owner of copyright the exclusive right to reproduce the copyrighted work, to prepare derivative works, to distribute copies of electronic media of the copyrighted work, to perform the copyrighted work publicly, or to display the copyrighted work publicly. The copyright protects the form of expression rather than the subject matter of the writing.

PATENTS

Constitutional and Statutory Authority

The Constitution of the United States gives Congress the power to enact laws relating to patents in Article I, section 8, which reads "Congress shall have power...to promote the progress of science and useful arts, by securing for limited times to authors and inventors the exclusive right to their respective writings and discoveries." Under this power, Congress has from time to time enacted various laws relating to patents. The first patent law was enacted in 1790. The law now in effect is a general revision that was enacted July 19, 1952, and that came into effect January 1, 1953. It is codified in Title 35, United States Code. The patent law specifies the subject matter for which a patent may be obtained and the conditions for patentability.

The law establishes the Patent and Trademark Office (PTO) to administer the law relating to the granting of patents and contains various other provisions relating to patents. The PTO is an agency of the U.S. Department of Commerce. Its role is to grant patents for the protection of inventions and to register trademarks. It serves the interest of inventors and businesses with respect to their inventions, corporate products, and service identifications. It also advises and assists the bureaus and offices of the Department of Commerce and other agencies of the government in matters involving intellectual property, such as patents, trademarks, and semiconductor mask works. Through the preservation, classification, and dissemination of patent information, the PTO aids and encourages innovation and the scientific and technical advancement of the nation.

In discharging its patent-related duties, the Patent and Trademark Office examines applications and grants patents on inventions when applicants are entitled to them; it publishes and disseminates patent information, records assignments of patents, maintains search files of U.S. and foreign patents, and maintains a search room for public use in examining issued patents and records. It supplies copies of patents and official records to the public. Similar functions are performed relating to trademarks.

What Can Be Patented

In the language of the statute, any person who invents or discovers any new and useful process, machine, manufacture, or composition or matter, or any new and useful improvement thereof, may obtain a patent, subject to the conditions and requirements of the law. The word *process* is defined by law as a process, act, or method, and primarily includes industrial or technical processes. The term *machine* as used in the statute needs no explanation. The term *manufacture* relates to chemical compositions and may include mixtures of ingredients as well as new chemical compounds. These classes of subject matter taken together include practically everything that is made by humans as well as the process for making the products.

The Atomic Energy Act of 1954 excludes the patenting of inventions useful solely in the utilization of special nuclear material or atomic energy for atomic weapons.

Patent law specifies that the subject matter must be useful. The term *useful* in this connection refers to the condition that the subject matter has a useful purpose and also includes operativeness, that is, a machine that will not operate to perform the intended purpose would not be called useful and, therefore, would not be granted a patent.

A patent cannot be obtained on a mere idea or suggestion. The patent is granted on the new machine, manufacture, and so on, as has been said, and not on the idea or suggestion of the new machine. A complete description of the actual machine or other subject matter for which a patent is sought is required.

Who May Apply for a Patent

According to the law, only the inventor may apply for a patent, with certain exceptions. If a person who is not the inventor should apply for a patent, the patent, if it were obtained, would be invalid. The person applying in such a case who falsely states that he/she is the inventor would also be subject to criminal penalties.

Specification (Description and Claims)

In framing an application for a patent, the following should be considered:

- Title of the invention.
- Background of the invention.
- Brief summary of the invention.
- Drawings (if any).

The specification must include a written description of the invention and the manner and process of making and using it; it is required to be in such full, clear, concise, and exact terms as to enable any person skilled in the technological area to which the invention pertains, or with which it is most nearly connected, to make and use the same.

The specification must set forth the precise invention for which a patent is solicited in such manner as to distinguish it from other inventions. It must describe completely a specific embodiment of the process, machine, manufacture, composition of matter, or improvement invented, and it must explain the mode of operation or principle whenever applicable.

The basic patent (utility) application fee is $690.00. However, fees may vary depending on the types of patent.

Patent Searches

The U.S. Patent and Trademark Office has a free, full-text patent database where patents can be searched. For example, if you want to search for William Quinn's patent, you can search by inventor:

IN/Quinn and IN/William

or, you can search by title:

TTL/thermal and TTL/switch

See Figures 4-1 and 4-2.

TRADEMARKS

Establishing Trademark Rights

Trademark rights arise from either (1) actual use of the mark, or (2) the filing of a proper application to register a mark in the PTO stating that the applicant has a bona fide intention to use the mark in commerce regulated by the U.S. Congress. Federal registration is not required to establish rights in a mark, nor is it required to begin use of a mark. However, federal registration can secure benefits beyond the rights acquired by merely using a mark. For example, the owner of a federal registration is presumed to be the owner of the mark for the goods and services specified in the registration and to be entitled to use the mark nationwide.

Two related but distinct types of rights in a mark are (1) the right to register and (2) the right to use. Generally, the first party who either uses a mark in commerce or files an application in the PTO has the ultimate right to register that mark. The PTO's authority is limited to determining the right to register. The right to use a mark can be more complicated to determine. This is particularly true when two parties have begun use of the same or similar marks without knowledge of one another and neither has a federal registration. Only a court can render a decision about the right to use, such as issuing an injunction or awarding damages for infringement.

Figure 4.1

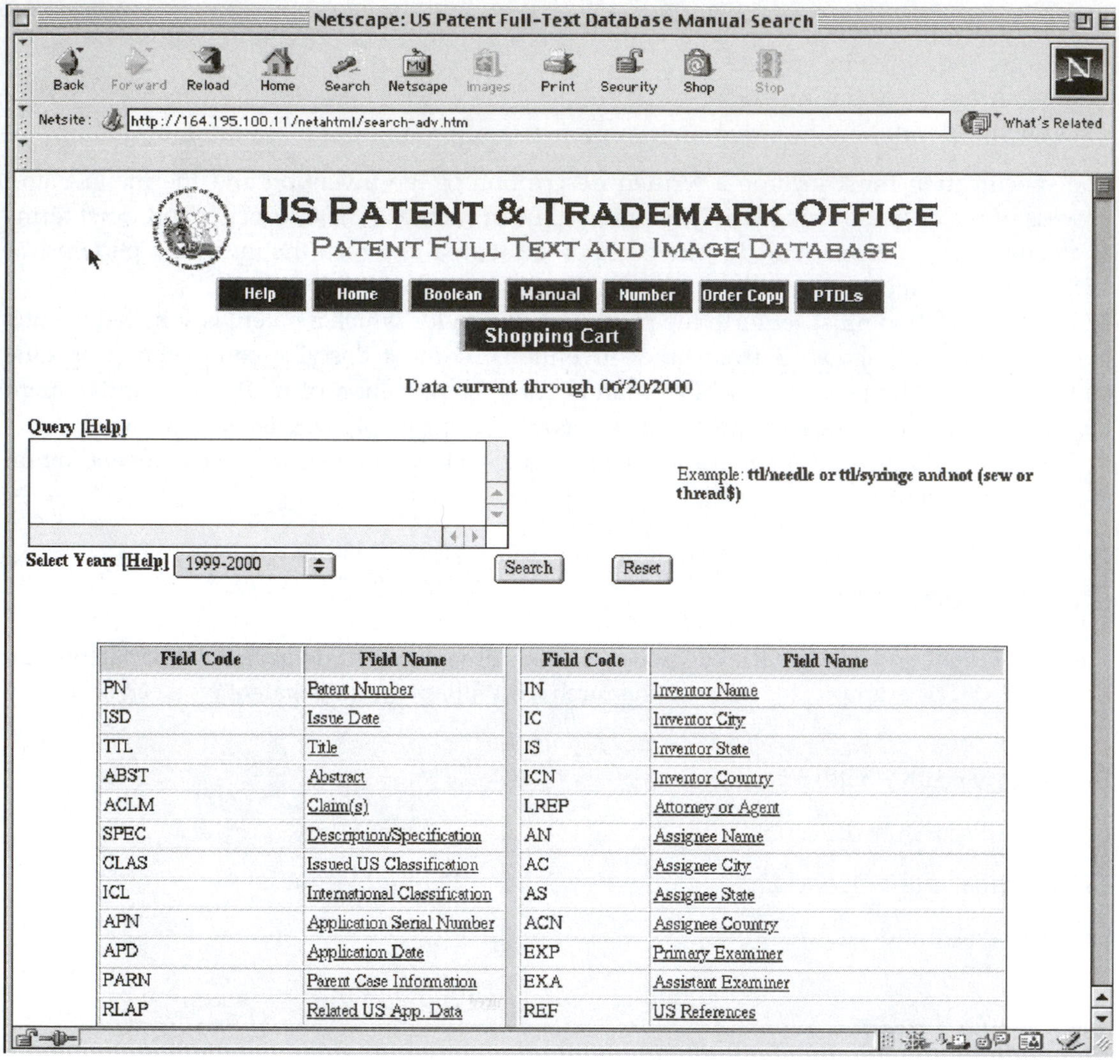

A federal registration can provide significant advantages to a party involved in a court proceeding. The PTO cannot provide advice concerning rights in a mark; only a private attorney can provide such advice.

Unlike copyrights or patents, trademark rights can last indefinitely if the owner continues to use the mark to identify its goods or services. The term of a federal trademark registration is 10 years, with 10-year renewal terms. However, between the fifth and sixth year after the date of initial registration, the registrant must file an affidavit setting forth certain information to keep the registration alive. If no affidavit is filed, the registration is canceled.

Figure 4.2

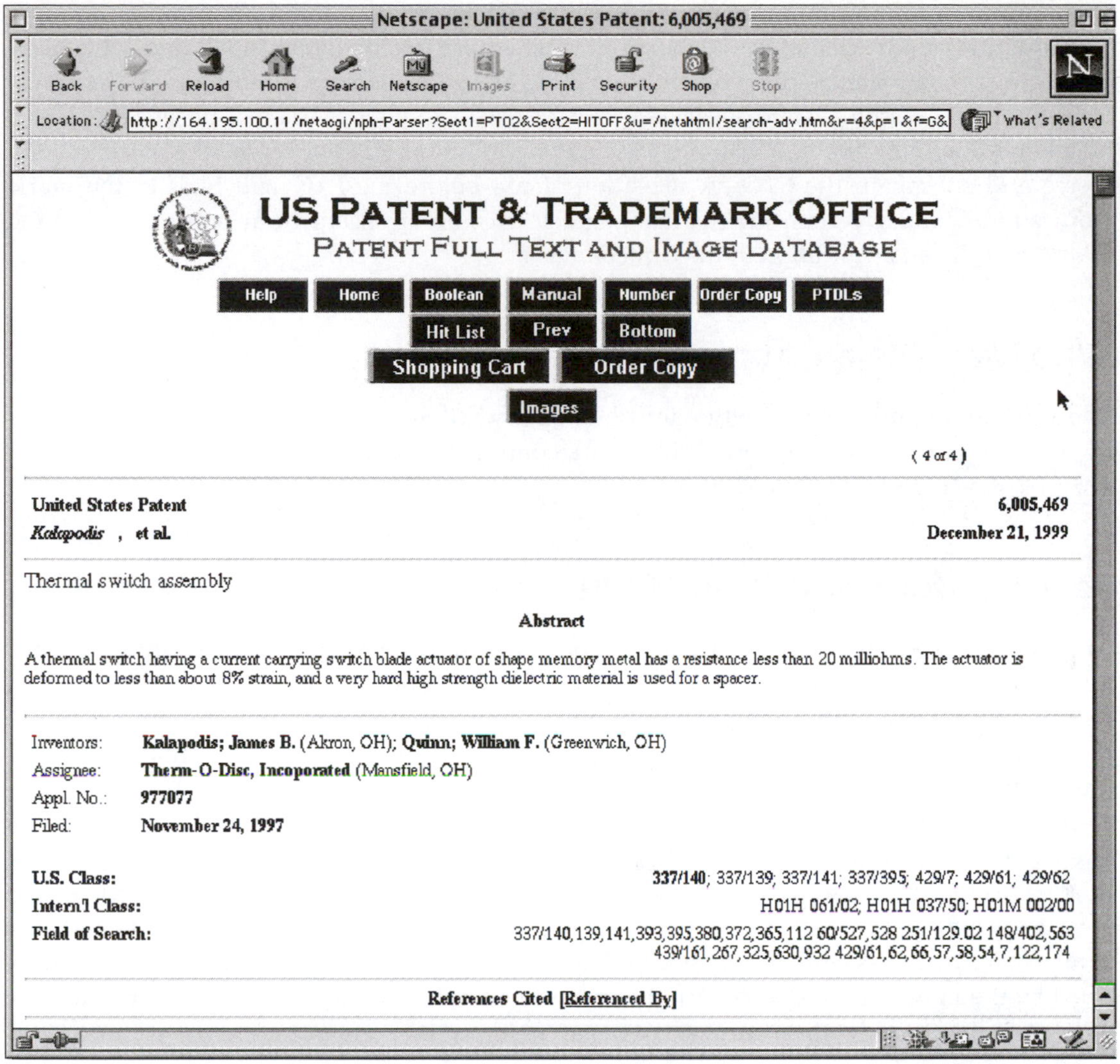

Types of Applications for Federal Registration

An applicant may apply for federal registration in two principal ways:

1. An applicant who has already commenced using a mark in commerce may file based on that use (a "use" application).
2. An applicant who has not yet used the mark may apply based on a bona fide intention to use the mark in commerce (an "intent-to-use" application).

For the purpose of obtaining federal registration, *commerce* means all commerce that may lawfully be regulated by the U.S. Congress, for example, interstate commerce or commerce between the United States and another country. The use in commerce must be a bona fide use in the ordinary course of trade and not made merely to reserve a right in a mark. Use of a mark in promotion or advertising before the product or service is actually provided under the mark on a normal commercial scale does not qualify as use in commerce. Use of a mark in purely local commerce within a state does not qualify as use in commerce. If an applicant files based on a bona fide intention to use in commerce, the applicant will have to use the mark in commerce and submit to the PTO an allegation of use before the PTO will register the mark. Additionally, under certain international agreements, an applicant from outside the United States may file an application in the United States.

Who May File an Application

The application must be filed in the name of the owner of the mark, usually an individual, corporation, or partnership. The owner of a mark controls the nature and quality of the goods or services identified by the mark.

Searches for Conflicting Marks

An applicant is not required to conduct a search for conflicting marks prior to applying with the PTO. However, some people find it useful. In evaluating an application, an examining attorney conducts a search and notifies the applicant if a conflicting mark is found. The application fee, which covers processing and search costs, will not be refunded even if a conflict is found and the mark cannot be registered.

To determine a conflict between two marks, the PTO determines whether there would be a likelihood of confusion, that is, whether relevant consumers would be likely to associate the goods or services of one party with those of the other party as a result of the use of the marks at issue by both parties. The principal factors to be considered in reaching this decision are the similarity of the marks and the commercial relationship between the goods and services identified by the marks. To find a conflict, the marks need not be identical, and the goods and services do not have to be the same.

Laws and Rules Governing Federal Registration

The federal registration of trademarks is governed by the Trademark Act of 1946, as amended, 15 U.S.C. §1051 et seq.; the Trademark Rules, 37 C.F.R. Part 2; and the Trademark Manual of Examining Procedure (2d ed., 1993).

Use of the ™, sm, and ® Symbols

Anyone who claims rights in a mark may use the ™ (trademark) or sm (service mark) designation with the mark to alert the public to the claim. It is not necessary to have a registration, or even a pending application, to use these designations. The claim may or may not be valid. The registration symbol, ®, may only be used when the mark is registered in the PTO. It is improper to use this symbol at any point before the registration issues.

COPYRIGHT

Copyright is a form of protection provided by the laws of the United States (Title 17, U.S. Code) to the authors of original works, including literary, dramatic, musical, artistic, and certain other intellectual works. This protection is available to both published and unpublished works. Section 106 of the 1976 Copyright Act generally gives the owner of copyright the exclusive right to do and to authorize others to do the following:

- To reproduce the work in copies of electronic media;
- To prepare derivative works based on the work;
- To distribute copies or phonorecords of the work to the public by sale or other transfer of ownership, or by rental, lease, or lending;
- To perform the work publicly, in the case of literary, musical, dramatic, and choreographic works, pantomimes, and motion pictures and other audiovisual works;
- To display the copyrighted work publicly, in the case of literary, musical, dramatic, and choreographic works, pantomimes, and pictorial, graphic, or sculptural works, including the individual images of a motion picture or other audiovisual work; and
- To perform the work publicly, in the case of sound recordings, by means of a digital audio transmission.

In addition, authors of certain works of visual art have the rights of attribution and integrity as described in section 106A of the 1976 Copyright Act.

It is illegal for anyone to violate any of the copyright holder's rights. These rights, however, are not unlimited in scope. Sections 107 through 121 of the 1976 Copyright Act establish limitations on these rights. In some cases, these limitations are a specified exemption from copyright liability. One major limitation is the doctrine of fair use, which is given a statutory basis in section 107 of the 1976 Copyright Act. In other instances, the limitation takes the form of a compulsory license under which certain limited uses of copyrighted works are permitted upon payment of specified royalties and compliance with statutory conditions. For further information about the limitations of any of these rights, consult the copyright law or write to the Copyright Office.

Who Can Claim Copyright

Copyright protection exists from the time the work is created in fixed form. The copyright in the work of authorship immediately becomes the property of the author who created the work. Only the author or those deriving their rights through the author can rightfully claim copyright.

In the case of works made for hire, the employer and not the employee is considered to be the author. Section 101 of the copyright law defines a "work made for hire" as

> a work prepared by an employee within the scope of his or her employment; or a work specially ordered or commissioned for use as a contribution to a collective work, as a part of a motion picture or other audiovisual work, as a translation, as a supplementary work, as a compilation, as an instructional text, as a test, as answer material for a test, or as an atlas, if the parties expressly agree in a written instrument signed by them that the work shall be considered a work made for hire.

The authors of a joint work are co-owners of the copyright in the work, unless there is an agreement to the contrary. Copyright in each separate contribution to a periodical or other collective work is distinct from copyright in the collective work as a whole and vests initially with the author of the contribution.

Two General Principles

1. Mere ownership of a book, manuscript, painting, or any other copy of phonorecord does not give the possessor the copyright. The law provides that transfer of ownership of any material object that embodies a protected work does not of itself convey any rights in the copyright.

2. Minors may claim copyright, but state laws may regulate the business dealings involving copyrights owned by minors. For information on relevant state laws, consult an attorney.

What Works Are Protected

Copyright protects original works of authorship that are fixed in a tangible form of expression. The fixation need not be directly perceptible so long as it may be communicated with the aid of a machine or device. Copyrightable works include the following categories:

- literary works
- musical works, including any accompanying words
- dramatic works, including any accompanying music
- pantomimes and choreographic works
- pictorial, graphic, and sculptural works
- motion pictures and other audiovisual works
- sound recordings
- architectural works

These categories should be viewed broadly. For example, computer programs and most compilations may be registered as literary works; maps and architectural plans may be registered as pictorial, graphic, and sculptural works.

What Is Not Protected by Copyright

Several categories of material are generally not eligible for federal copyright protection. These include, among others:

- Works that have not been fixed in a tangible form of expression (for example, choreographic works that have not been notated or recorded, or improvisational speeches or performances that have not been written or recorded).
- Titles, names, short phrases, and slogans; familiar symbols or designs; mere variations of typographic ornamentation, lettering, or coloring; mere listings of ingredients or contents.
- Ideas, procedures, methods, systems processes, concepts, principles, discoveries, or devices, as distinguished from a description, explanation, or illustration.
- Works consisting entirely of information that is common property and containing no original authorship (for example, standard calendars, height and weight charts, tape measures and rules, and lists or tables taken from public documents or other common sources).

How to Secure a Copyright

The way in which copyright protection is secured is frequently misunderstood. No publication or registration or other action in the Copyright Office is required to secure copyright. There are, however, certain definite advantages to registration. Copyright is secured automatically when the work is created, and a work is created when it is fixed in a copy or phonorecord for the first time. Copies are material objects from which a work can be read or visually perceived either directly or with the aid of a machine or device, such as books, manuscripts, sheet music, film, videotape, or microfilm. Phonorecords are material objects embodying fixation of sounds (excluding, by statutory definition, motion picture soundtracks), such as cassette tapes, CDs, or LPs. Thus, for example, a song (the "work") can be fixed in sheet music ("copies") or in phonograph disks ("phonorecords"), or both.

If a work is prepared over time, the part of the work that is fixed on a particular date constitutes the created work as of that date.

Publication

Publication is no longer the key to obtaining federal copyright as it was under the Copyright Act of 1909. However, publication remains important to copyright owners. The 1976 Copyright Act defines publication as the distribution of copies or phonorecords of a work. The copyright notice should be affixed to copies or phonorecords in such a way as to give reasonable notice of the claim of copyright. The elements of the notice should ordinarily appear together on the copies or phonorecords or on the phonorecord label or container. The Copyright Office has issued regulations concerning the form and position of the copyright notice in the Code of Federal Regulations (37 C.F.R. Part 202.20). For more information, request Circular 3, Copyright Notice.

How Long Copyright Protection Endures

A work that is created (fixed in tangible form for the first time) on or after January 1, 1978, is automatically protected from the moment of its creation and is ordinarily given a term enduring for the author's life plus an additional 70 years after the author's death.

Copyright Registration

Registration may be made at any time within the life of the copyright. Unlike the law before 1978, when a work has been registered in unpublished form, it is not necessary to make another registration when the work becomes published, although the copyright owner may register the published edition, if desired.

- If the work was first published in the United States on or after January 1, 1978, two complete copies or phonorecords of the work as first published are needed.
- If sending multiple works, all applications, deposits, and fees should be sent in the same package. If possible, applications should be attached to the appropriate deposit. Whenever possible, number each package (e.g., 1 of 3) to facilitate processing.

Effective Date of Registration

A copyright registration is effective on the date the Copyright Office receives all the required elements in acceptable form, regardless of how long it then takes to process the application and mail the certificate of registration. The time the Copyright Office requires to process an application varies, depending on the amount of material the office is receiving.

> **HINT**
>
> Cut out extra time and money. You can do a patent or trademark search for free on the U.S. Patent & Trademark Website: http://www.uspto.gov.

WHERE TO BEGIN

For an overview of patents, trademarks, and copyright, begin with Arthur Miller's *Intellectual Property—Patents, Trademarks, and Copyright in a Nutshell*, or with Jay Dratler's *Intellectual Property Law: Commercial, Creative, and Industrial Property*. (See the bibliography following this explanation.) Loose-leaf services such as *Chisum on Patents, Lindey on Entertainment, Publishing, and the Arts, Milgrim on Licensing*, and *Nimmer on Copyright* provide the latest information, including case law, rules and regulations, forms, and new developments. Westlaw and Lexis have both patent and trademark databases. The U.S. Patent and Trademark Office has its own Website, and the U.S. Copyright Office has its own home page.

BIBLIOGRAPHY

Loose-Leaf Services

CCH Copyright Law Reports. Chicago, Ill.: Commerce Clearing House, 1999. This publication gives guidance on protection of intellectual property; it has explanations and full-text reporting of federal and state copyright law, reference materials, new developments, and court decisions. *Copyright Law Reports* also includes case tables. *CCH Copyright Law Decisions* comes along with the *Copyright Law Reporter*. The decisions contain archived and new information on case law, along with information that is in the *Copyright Law Reports*. KF 2991.5 .C6.

Chisum on Patents: A Treatise on the Law of Patentability, Validity, and Infringement. New York: Matthew Bender, 1999. This publication covers all aspects of patent law and related issues. Chisum also has thorough coverage of the substantive law-principles, doctrines, rules, and cases. KF 3114 .C47.

Alexander Lindey. *Lindey on Entertainment, Publishing, and the Arts: Agreements and the Law*. Deerfield, Ill.: Clark Boardman Callaghan, 1980. This is a loose-leaf service with coverage of sound recordings, computer software, music video programming, motion pictures, books, magazines, and plays. KF 2992 .L5.

Roger M. Milgrim. *Milgrim on Licensing*. New York: Matthew Bender, 1999. This loose-leaf service has an emphasis on license agreements, patent licenses, and technology transfer. KF 3145 .M55.

Melville Dimmer. *Dimmer on Copyright: A Treatise on the Law of Literary, Musical, and Artistic Property and Protection of Ideas*. New York: Matthew Bender, 1999. This loose-leaf service includes a variety of topics, such as wide-ranging software, liability of online service providers for copyright infringement, and international copyright protection. KG 2991.5 .N5.

Treatises

Jay Drawler. *Intellectual Property Law: Commercial, Creative, and Industrial Property*. New York: Law Journal Seminars Press, 1991. This publication includes a foundation on intellectual property, as well as bibliographic references and an index. IF 2979.D73.

Illustrated Texts

John Mendenhall. *High Tech Trademarks*. New York: Art Direction Book Company, 1988. This is chiefly an illustrated text on trademarks. T 325 .M46.

Kuwayama Isobar. *Trademarks and Symbols of the World*. Rockport, Mass.: Rockport Publishers, 1988. This is a 3-volume, illustrated book of trademarks and symbols of the world. T 325 .K913.

Case Law

U.S. Patents Quarterly. Washington, D.C.: Associated Industry Publications, 1999. This publication reports cases relating to patents, trademarks, and copyrights. It cumulates the *United States Patents Quarterly* (serial) and also contains weekly advance sheets. IF 2975.3 .B8.

Nutshells

Arthur R. Miller and Michael H. Davis. *Intellectual Property—Patents, Trademarks and Copyright in a Nutshell*. 2nd ed. St. Paul, Minn.: West, 1990. IF 2980.M52 1990.

Computer Sources

Westlaw

FIP-PTO (patent and trademark decisions)
FIP-TM (U.S. trademarks)
WPI (Derwent Word Product Index)

Lexis

LEXPAT;ABSTCL (abstracts and claims)
PATENT;PTO (combined courts and Board of Patent Appeals cases)
PATENT;FEDCTS (federal courts)

Internet Sites

U.S. Copyright Home Office Page: http://lcweb.loc.gov/copyright
U.S. Trademarks: http://www.uspto.gov and http://www.ggmark.com/
IBM Intellectual Property Network: http://www.patents.ibm.com
For intellectual property, search: http://www.ipmag.com

ENDNOTES

1. All material was taken from the U.S. Patent and Trademark Website: http://www.uspto.gov.

ASSIGNMENT A

Patents/Trademarks/Copyright Research

Sources

Nimmer on Copyright: A Treatise on the Law of Literary, Musical, and Artistic Property, and Protection of Ideas
Chisum on Patents: A Treatise on the Law of Patentability, Validity, and Infringement
Lindey on Entertainment, Publishing, and the Arts: Agreements and the Law

1. Using *Nimmer on Copyright*, look under musical compositions, sound recordings, and find out if a musical composition and a sound recording may be registered together on a single application.

2. Again, using *Nimmer*, are tapes, cassette tapes, and cartridge disks sound recordings?

3. Look at *Chisum on Patents*. Is a sheet of music—printed matter—within the statutory classes of patentable subject matter, that is, printed matter on an eligible claim?

4. Look up the Trademark Act of 1946 (Lantham Act) in *Lindey on Entertainment*, Volume 5, Appendix H. How does the owner of a trademark apply to register his or her trademark?

ASSIGNMENT B

Patents/Trademarks/Copyright Research

1. Go to U.S. Copyright Office home page on the Internet. The address is:

   http://lcweb.loc.gov/copyright

   Go to the PTO Forms section and find the Patent Application Data Entry Format: Guide for Preparing Bibliographic Data for Electronic Capture. What three types of information must every applicant provide?

2. Search the U.S. Trademark Browse Serve on the Internet:

   http://wwwl.uspto.gov

   Go to the "U.S. Trademark Combined Marks Search" and search for the "Mickey Mouse" trademark. Check Mickey Mouse, Serial Number 71-266717. What is the owner's address in Burbank?

3. Do a trademark search to see if there is a trademark for "inshredible" (regarding men's and women's clothing). On Westlaw (through Dialog), search:

   FIP-TM* (Federal Intellectual Property—Trademarkscan—active marks)

   (as the database). *(Westlaw) (Dialog) may charge for this search.

   Search:

   TR (shred! Credib! Edibl! & ic(003 014 023 024 025 026 035 044)

   (ic = international code)

   Also try:

   MIP-TM (State Trademarks) (as the database)

   Search:

   Inshred! Shred & ic (003 014 023 025 026 035 044)

   You can also search on Lexis:*

   TRDMRK;ALLTM (Federal Trademarks Library and All Trademarks File)

   TRDMRK;STTM (State Trademarks Library and All Trademarks File)

   *Lexis may charge (by the item) for this search. Or you can search for free: http://www.uspto.gov (the U.S. Patent & Trademark Office Website).

Does a trademark for "inshredible" exist? What are some of the marks that exist?

4. Find West's Legal Forms. Locate the volume with "Patents, Trademarks, and Copyrights," and find a form for a Declaration and Power of Attorney for a Design Patent Application.

CHAPTER 5

Employment/Labor Law

INTRODUCTION

The industrialization of the American economy in the years after 1865 resulted in an enormous increase in the labor force.[1] Working conditions and pay scales were poor, resulting in attempts to organize bargaining units. These first efforts were crushed by the depression of 1830. A second spurt of organization in the 1850s was not successful.

The Knights of Labor developed in the 1880s. Their practice of open membership led to much internal strife, and by 1890, this organization had declined. This group was the first to accept capitalization and to use collective bargaining. In 1886, with a membership of 250,000, the national craft unions formed the American Federation of Labor (AFL). By 1914, membership in the AFL exceeded 2,000,000. Legal bickering between unions and powerful industry forces led to the passage of the Sherman Antitrust Act of 1890. As it turned out, the first use of these antitrust provisions were against the unions.

The Pullman Strike of 1893 focused legal attention on, and resulted in, the appointment of the U.S. Strike Commission, followed the Erdman Act of l898. This act was not effective and was eventually declared to be unconstitutional by the U.S. Supreme Court.

The Clayton Act of 1914 was hailed as a laborers' Magna Carta, because the act banned the use of antitrust laws against labor unions and barred the use of federal injunctions in disputes between employers and employees. In 1921, the Supreme Court handed down two separate decisions that all but destroyed the effectiveness of the Clayton Act.

From 1914 until World War I, labor made some gains. The Wilson administration tried to prevent labor disputes by establishing a National War Labor Board. This board vigorously backed the right of unions to organize and to bargain collectively. Next came the Railway Labor Act (RLA) of 1926, which ruled for compulsory arbitration, imposing a duty on both sides to negotiate and creating a Mediation Board. The Supreme Court has upheld the RLA and amended the act to apply to airlines. The Railway Labor Act has remained a part of collective bargaining until the present time.

The AFL was an affiliation of many diverse unions. It did not, however, organize all workers in a given area. This practice led to serious disagreements within the union itself. During the 1935 convention, a group, headed by John L. Lewis, withdrew from the AFL and formed the Committee of Industrial Organizations (CIO). The CIO was plagued by Communist disputes. When Walter Router of the CIO and George Meany of the AFL found common ground, the two organizations merged into the new AFL-CIO confederation.

Present labor law is based on four major pieces of federal legislation: the Norris-La Guardia Act of 1932, the National Labor Relations Act of 1935, the Labor Management Relations Act of 1947, and the Landrum-Griffin Act of 1959.

The Norris-LaGuardia Act of 1932

Prior to 1930, union organizing and collective bargaining were impeded by such industrial practices as Yellow Dog contracts, objective tests, vicarious responsibility, and many types of injunctions. The Norris-LaGuardia Act removed the power of federal courts to enjoin normal union activity. At the same time, the act guaranteed the right of workers to negotiate the terms and conditions of their employment. Judicial response to the act was that legitimate labor activities were exempt from the federal antitrust laws.

The National Labor Relations Act of 1935

The National Labor Relations Act (NLRA) guaranteed employees the freedom to form, join, or assist labor organizations; the freedom to bargain collectively with their employers; and the right to engage in concerted activities for mutual aid and protection. The NLRA also imposed obligations on employers to bargain in good faith. The act immediately came under attack by industry. However, the courts rejected all arguments and upheld the constitutionality of the NLRA.

The Labor Management Relations Act of 1947

By 1947, union membership had increased to about fifteen million workers. Industrywide strikes and the actions of labor bosses, such as John. L Lewis, enraged the general public. The Congressional response to these factors was to pass the Labor Management Relations Act (LMRA). Organized labor bitterly opposed this act, because it allowed legislative interference in labor disputes; the LMRA set a prohibition against unfair labor practices, opened the closed shop, limited the terms of pension funds, and provided legal means of enforcement of labor agreements.

The Labor Management Reporting and Disclosure Act of 1959 (the Landrum-Griffin Act)

During the 1950s, senate investigations into union practices uncovered corruption and lack of democratic procedures in many unions. The Landrum-Griffin Act was passed to impose some regulation on internal affairs of unions and to set a bill of rights for union members.

Title VII of the Civil Rights Act of 1964

Title VII of the Civil Rights Act of 1964 (Title VII-42 U.S.C. §2000(e), et seq) as amended by the Equal Opportunity Act of 1972, makes it unlawful for an employer

- To fail or refuse to hire or to discharge any individual or otherwise to discriminate against any individual, with respect to his or her compensation in terms, conditions, or privileges of employment because of that individual's race, color, religion, sex, or national origin; or
- To limit, segregate, or classify employees or applicants for employment in any way that would deprive or tend to deprive any individual of employment opportunities or otherwise affect status as an employee because of the individual's race, color, religion, sex, national origin; or
- To discriminate against any individual based on opposition to any employment practice unlawful under Title VII because of the filing of a charge of discrimination or participation in a Title VII proceeding.

Title VII applies to employment agencies and labor organizations, as well as to employers. It covers all forms of discrimination in all aspects of the employment relationship, dealing with permanent employment as well as training programs. Under the 1978 amendments, the prohibition against sex discrimination includes discrimination based on pregnancy, childbirth, or related medical conditions.

Under Title VII, an employer covered under the act is any person "engaged in an industry affecting commerce and which employer has fifteen or more employees for each working day in each of twenty or more calendar weeks in the current or preceding calendar year, and any agent of such person."

There are exceptions to Title VII. Conditions of employment are permitted if the plan is formulated in good faith with no intent to evade the law. Such exceptions include those pertaining to seniority, merit, or incentive systems; professionally developed tests; bona fide occupational qualifications (female models for women's clothing); and discrimination against communists, aliens, or in the interest of national security.

Employees who feel that they have been discriminated against can file a claim with the Equal Employment Opportunity Commission (EEOC). To file such a complaint, the charges must be in writing and must be made under oath affirmation. The EEOC must serve notice of the charge on the party being charged within 10 days of its receipt of the charge. The EEOC then investigates the charge to determine whether there is "reasonable cause to believe that the charge is true." The EEOC gathers facts; the charge may be settled or dismissed during the fact-finding process.

When a charge has not been settled or dismissed and fact finding is concluded, the EEOC makes a determination whether reasonable cause exists. If there is a no-cause finding, the commission will close its case and issue a notice of right-to-sue letter to the charging party, permitting him or her to file suit in federal court on the charge. If the EEOC makes a finding that there is reasonable cause, it will attempt to conciliate the dispute and have the employer agree to end any unfair employment practice. If an agreement is reached, it is signed by all parties. If conciliation is unsuccessful, either the charging party or the EEOC may bring suit.

An individual may bring a suit in U.S. District Court under Title VII if he or she has filed a timely charge with the EEOC, has received a notice of right to sue, and files his or her own suit within 90 days of receipt of the notice of the right to sue. The EEOC may itself bring suit on a certain charge. This charge precludes the individual from suing, although he or she may join the EEOC's action.

The plaintiff in an action brought under Title VII bears the ultimate burden of proving that the employer discriminated against him or her on the basis of the employee being a member of a protected group. The plaintiff may satisfy this burden either by producing direct evidence or intentional discrimination or by circumstantial evidence. Remedies for the plaintiff may include enjoining the employer from engaging in such unlawful employment practices and ordering reinstatement of the employee, with or without back pay.

Where to Begin

To research a Title VII or other labor/employment matter, check in the federal statutes, preferably U.S.C.A. or U.S.C.S. as opposed to U.S.C., to find the text of the statute (see the bibliography following this commentary). Both of the annotated statutes are easier to use than the United States Code (U.S.C.) because the annotated versions of the statutes have better indexes, have finding tools, and are easier to read. For Title VII, look under 42 U.S.C. §2000(e) et seq. (and continuing). For the relevant state laws, check state statutes.

Mack Player's nutshell publication called *Federal Law of Employment Discrimination in a Nutshell*, or his hornbook, *Employment Discrimination*, can give a good overview of employment law, including Title VII. Loose-leaf services, including the *BNA Fair Employment Guide* or the *CCH Employment Practices Guide*, offer complete coverage of both state and federal laws, decisions, and rulings. For case law, *CCH Labor Cases* has a wealth of information. Westlaw offers a variety of databases, including National Mediation Board Decisions, Employees Compensation Planning Portfolios, among many others. On the Internet, there is a specific site for employment discrimination: http://www.law.cornell.edu.

HINT

The *BNA Labor Relations Reporter* will save you time and money, because this handy loose-leaf has everything in one place—court decisions, arbitration awards, recommendations of fact-finding boards, and decisions of the National Wage Stabilization Board.

BIBLIOGRAPHY

Loose-Leaf Services

BNA Fair Employment Practice Cases. Washington, D.C.: Bureau of National Affairs, 1999. This 100-volume loose-leaf service contains opinions of federal and state courts and administrative agencies under federal and state laws relating to employment discrimination based on race, color, creed, sex, national origin, or age. This publication contains a cumulative digest, index, and table of cases. KF 3315 .L324.

BNA Labor Arbitration Reports. Washington, D.C.: Bureau of National Affairs, 1999. This publication deals with awards of arbitration, recommendations of fact-finding boards, court decisions on labor arbitration, and decisions of the National Wage Stabilization Board. The *Labor Arbitration Reports* is a 100-volume loose-leaf that has a cumulative digest and an index with a table of cases. KF 3315 .L44.

BNA Labor Relations Reporter. Washington, D.C.: Bureau of National Affairs, 1999. This publication covers the Americans with Disabilities Act, fair employment practices, individual employment rights, labor arbitration, labor—management relations, state laws, and wages and hours. This publication has decisions of the National Labor Relations Board (NLRB) and of the courts, with a cumulative digest, index, and table of cases. KF 3302 .L34.

CCH Employment Practices Guide. Chicago, Ill.: Commerce Clearing House, 1999. This publication offers complete coverage of both state and federal antidiscrimination laws and has the full text of employment discrimination decisions and rulings, and federal and state antidiscrimination laws. The guide also includes explanations, forms, and a bimonthly newsletter. KF 3464 .A6C6.

CCH Labor Arbitration Awards. Chicago, Ill.: Commerce Clearing House, 1999. This comprehensive resource gives fast reporting of pertinent labor arbitration awards setting everyday and dispute situations. Reported awards cover representative industries from various geographical areas of the country and reflect grievances of wide interest. This report includes arbitrator biographies, tables of awards by party and arbitrator, principal labor unions, and a list of arbitrators by state. KF 3421 .C6.

Arthur Larson and Lex K. Larson. *Employment Discrimination*. New York: Matthew Bender, 1988. This publication carries comprehensive coverage that keeps pace with the continuing evolution of the law relating to employment discrimination based on race, sex, religion, national origin, age, disability, and union membership. KF 3464 .L37.

Case Law

CCH Labor Cases. Chicago, Ill.: Commerce Clearing House, 1999. This publication is a selective reporter of decisions rendered by federal and state courts throughout the United States on federal and state labor problems, with case tables and topical indexes. KF 3315 .L42.

CD-ROMs

CCH Unemployment Insurance Reporter. (CD-ROM). Chicago, Ill.: Commerce Clearing House, 1999. This CD-ROM provides monthly reporting of new developments and information on Social Security, Federal Unemployment Insurance, and State Unemployment Insurance. It also contains regulations, judicial and administrative decisions, rulings, releases, and forms. KF 3673.4 .C6.

Hornbooks

Harold S. Lewis. *Civil Rights and Employment Discrimination Law*. St. Paul, Minn.: West, 1997. KF 3464 .L486 1997.

Mack A. Player. *Employment Discrimination Law*. St. Paul, Minn.: West, 1988. KF 3464 .P58 1988b.

Nutshell

Mack A. Player. *Federal Law of Employment Discrimination in a Nutshell*. 4th ed. St. Paul, Minn.: West, 1999. KF 3464.Z9 .P55 1999.

Statutes

Civil Rights Act of 1964, 42 U.S.C. §21
Equal Pay Act of 1963, 29 U.S.C. §206
Americans with Disabilities Act of 1990, 42 U.S.C. §126
The Age Discrimination in Employment Act, 29 U.S.C. §§621–634
The Rehabilitation Act, 29 U.S.C. §791, 793, 794(a)

Computer Sources

Westlaw

LRR-DIR (BNA Labor Relations Reporter—list of arbitrators)
LA-COMB (BNA Labor Relations Reporter decisions—state and federal)
FLB-ECAB (Employees' Compensation Appeals Board Decisions)
FLB-WHOL (Wage and Opinion Letters)
FLB-NMB (National Mediation Board Decisions)
EB-INFO (Dialog) (Employee Benefits Infosource)

Lexis

BNA;LRRFEP (Labor Relations Reporter)
EMPLOY;LRRFEP
LABOR;SSRULE (Social Security Rulings)

LABOR;TNCPP (Tax Management Compensation Planning Portfolios)
LABOR;NMB (National Mediation Board)
LABOR;ECAB (Employee Compensation Appeals Board)

Internet Sites

For employment discrimination, search: http://www.law.cornell.edu.

ENDNOTES

1. This section is based on Michael F. Marino and John C. Unkovic, *Labor and Employment in Pennsylvania: A Guide to Employment Laws, Regulations, and Practices* (Boston: Butterworth Legal Publishers, 1997).

ASSIGNMENT A

Employment/Labor Research

Sources

BNA *Fair Employment Cases*
Shepard's Act and Cases by Popular Name
U.S.C.A/U.S.C.S.
Westlaw
Lexis

Your client, a disgruntled ex-employee and civil servant, is suing her former employer because her dismissal was retaliatory since she turned in her employer on sex discrimination charges. She wants to know if there is liability under the Whistleblower statute. Moreover, she wants to know if punitive damages are allowed for malicious attempts to punish an employee who attempted to advance public policy. Cite appropriate statutory and case law.

1. First, look in *Shepard's Acts and Cases by Popular Name* or in the index to the *U.S.C.A/ U.S.C.S.* to find a cite for the Whistleblower Protection Act. (Note: On Westlaw, the database is USCA, and on Lexis, the Library and file are GENFED;USCS.)

   You will find a range of sections under the title. In particular, look under Whistleblower Protection Act Prohibited Personnel Practices. What is the appropriate U.S. Code section? Cite the section.

   Now search in Westlaw in FLB-CS (Federal Labor Cases), or on Lexis, LABOR-ECAB, for the Whistleblower Protection Act to find *Tucker v. Health and Human Services*. (Hint: If you "di" (for digest) before your search and put your search terms in parentheses, your search will retrieve a result that digests the editor's headnotes.)

2. Now look in the BNA *Fair Employment Practice Cases Cumulative Digest and Index with Table of Cases*, under "Sex Discrimination," and find the *Hallquist* case. (Hint: Look under "Discharge, Termination in General.") What did *Hallquist* hold?

3. Concerning punitive damages, find a District Court of Alabama case and cite it. What did the case hold? Look in the *Fair Employment Practice Cases* (under Punitive Damages) to see if punitive damages are allowed. Cite the case.

ASSIGNMENT B

Employment Law Research

Sources

Lexis
Westlaw
Shepard's Acts and Cases by Popular Name
U.S.C.A. or U.S.C.S.
Treatises
Black's Law Dictionary

1. Find a definition of self-employed. (Hint: Try the GENFED;NEWER Library and File, or the LABOR Library and COURTS File on Lexis. Westlaw has ALLFEDS or FLB-ALL. On Lexis, there is a search for definitions—self-employ! w/15 defin! or mean! or interp! or construe! or construed! A similar search can be used on Westlaw: self-employ! /15 defin! mean! interp! construe! construed!)

   First, find a case that defines self-employed. Then modify your search to find the case that held that when a union strikes to promote enlarged membership, Congress can prohibit a union from resorting to a secondary boycott or can prohibit self-employed persons from joining.

2. Use Westlaw or Lexis and find out what a Ponzi scheme is. Use the same type as in question 1. Also, find an appropriate article referencing Ponzi schemes.

3. What is the National Labor Relations Act? Look in *Black's Law Dictionary* or online. What is the appropriate U.S. Code section for this act? What is a relevant treatise that discusses the act?

CHAPTER 6

Securities

INTRODUCTION

A security is defined in §2(1) of the Securities Act of 1933 to include "any note, stock, treasury stock, bond, debenture, evidence of indebtedness, certificate of interest of participation in any profit-sharing agreement, collateral-trust certificate, transferable share, investment contract, certificate of deposit...or any instrument commonly known as a security, or any certificate for receipt, guarantee of, or right to subscribe to any of the foregoing."

Securities have distinctive features:

1. Securities are created, rather than produced, and can be issued in unlimited amounts, virtually without cost.[1]
2. Securities are not used or consumed by their purchasers—they are a kind of currency.[2]
3. Because the trading markets for securities are uniquely susceptible to manipulative and deceptive practices, all securities laws contain general anti-fraud provisions.[3]
4. Because a large industry has developed to buy and sell securities for investors and traders, securities laws are concerned with the regulation of people and firms engaged in that business to ensure that they do not take advantage of their superior experience and access to overreach their nonprofessional customers.[4]
5. Securities laws provide for a variety of governmental sanctions against those who violate their prohibitions, as well as civil liability to persons injured by such violations.[5]

Publicly held securities in the United States are traded both on formal securities exchanges and in the more loosely organized "over-the-counter" markets.[6] The largest and most prestigious national exchange is the New York Stock Exchange, which is followed both in size and in prestige by the American Stock Exchange.[7] Both of these national exchanges are recognized and regulated pursuant to section 6 of the Securities Exchange Act of 1934 and thus are subject to supervision and oversight by the Securities and Exchange Commission.[8] The exchanges provide investor protection through the minimum standards for securities as imposed by their listing requirements and also through their requirements for broker-dealer membership.[9] In addition to the two national exchanges, there are eight regional exchanges: the Boston Stock Exchange, the Chicago Board Options Exchange, the Inter-Mountain Exchange, the Cincinnati Exchange, the Midwest Stock Exchange, the Pacific Stock Exchange, the Philadelphia Stock Exchange, and the Spokane Stock Exchange.[10] Many of the securities on the regional exchanges are also traded on the New York Stock Exchange.[11]

The largest number of issuers have their securities traded on the over-the-counter markets, although exchange-listed securities generally have greater trading volume or turnover.[12]

Unlike the national exchanges, the over-the-counter markets merely provide a forum for brokers and dealers to arrange their own securities trades.[13] Much of the trading on over-the-counter markets has been facilitated by the National Association of Securities Dealers Automated Quotation System (NASDAQ).[14]

Most of the day-to-day trading on both the securities exchanges and the over-the-counter markets consists of transactions between investors and involve securities that have previously been issued by the corporation or other issuer. All of the proceeds from these sales, after commissions to the brokers, go to the private investors who are parting with their securities. This aspect of securities markets is referred to as trading and is regulated primarily by the provisions of the Securities and Exchange Act of 1934.[15] The process by which securities are first offered to the public, frequently referred to as distributions, is governed primarily by the Securities Act (SA) of 1933.[16] Registration of securities is also required under the Securities Act of 1933.[17]

The act that is directed in regulating all aspects of public trading of securities is the Securities Exchange Act (SEA) of 1934.[18] This act also has special provisions dealing with stock manipulation, improper trading, insider trading, and misstatements in filing.[19]

Following the Securities Exchange Act of 1934, Congress enacted the Public Utility Holding Company Act (PUHCA) of 1935, which deals with the problems raised when financing public issue utilities; the Trust Indenture Act (TIA) of 1939, which deals with debt financing of public issue; and the Investment Company Act (ICA) of 1940 and Investment Advisers Act (IAA) of 1940, which regulate mutual funds.[20]

The Securities and Exchange Commission

The Securities and Exchange Commission is a supervisory agency consisting of five commissioners serving 5-year terms, is appointed by the President, and is confirmed by Congress.[21] The full commission, in addition to exercising its supervisory power over all its divisions, has direct review power of rulings and hearings before an administrative judge, as well as the final authority on the promulgation of all SEC rules.[22] Regional offices of the SEC are located in New York, Boston, Atlanta, Chicago, Fort Worth, Denver, Los Angeles, Seattle, and Philadelphia.

HINT

Save time and energy: The *CCH Securities Law Reporter* is the most comprehensive and convenient source for all the federal securities laws, SEC rules, forms, interpretations and decisions, and court decisions on federal matters.

BIBLIOGRAPHY

Loose-Leaf Services

Federal Securities Law Reporter. Chicago, Ill.: Commerce Clearing House, 1999. This 7-volume loose-leaf is the most current source for securities materials, including laws, regulations, forms, rulings, policy decisions, and decisions. KF 1436.5 .C646.

Securities Regulation and Law Report. Washington, D.C.: Bureau of National Affairs, 1999. This publication is a weekly summary of federal and state securities developments. KF 1436 .S4.

Blue Sky Reporter. Chicago, Ill.: Commerce Clearing House, 1999. This is the most comprehensive source for the statutes, regulations, and decisions of the various states. This publication also has a section on the Uniform Securities Act and a section on uniform forms. KF 1068.4 .B58.

Hornbooks

Thomas Lee Hazen. *The Law of Securities Regulation*. St. Paul, Minn.: West, 1997. KF 1439 .H39 1990.

Harry G. Henn and John R. Alexander. *Laws of Corporations and Other Business Enterprises*. 3rd ed. St. Paul, Minn.: West, 1983 with 1986 pocket part. KF 1414 .H45 1983b.

Alan A. Palmiter. *Securities Regulation: Examples and Explanations*. New York: Aspen Publishers, 1998. KF 1440 .P25.

Lewis D. Solomon and Alan R. Palmiter. *Corporations: Examples and Explanations*. 3rd ed. New York: Aspen Publishers, 1999. KF 1418 .S65 1999.

Nutshells

Robert W. Hamilton. *The Law of Corporations in a Nutshell*. 4th ed. St. Paul, Minn.: West, 1996. KF 1414.3 .H35 1996.

David L. Ratner. *Securities Regulation in a Nutshell*. 6th ed. St. Paul, Minn.: West, 1998. KF 1440 .R37.

Administrative Decisions

SEC Docket. Chicago, Ill.: Commerce Clearing House, Exchange Commission, 1999. This is a weekly compilation of SEC releases, which are orders, notices, proposed rules, and rules. KF SE 1.29.

SEC Today. Washington, D.C.: Washington Service Bureau, 1999. This is a daily news publication that includes the SEC News Digest. KF 1444 .S22.

Treatises

Louis Loss. *Fundamentals of Securities Regulation*. Boston: Little, Brown, 1995. KF 1439 .I68.

Statutes

Securities Act of 1933, 15 U.S.C. §77(a)–77(m)
Securities Exchange Act of 1934, 15 U.S.C. §78(a)–78(kk)

C.F.R.

17 C.F.R. §230 (1933 Act)
17 C.F.R. §240 (1934 Act)

Computer Sources

Westlaw

SEC10Q (Dialog)
SEC-10K (Dialog)
SEC-AR (annual reports) (Dialog)
FSEC-NAL (no-action letters)
SEC-PROXY (Dialog)
FSEC-DIG (Security News Digest)
SECBLUE (Blue Sky Law)
CCH-USTC
FSEC-CS (Cases)

Lexis

COMPNY;10Q
FEDSEC;10K
COMPNY;ARS
FEDSEC;NOACT
COMPNY;PROXY
FEDSEC;SECREL(Releases)
CHSEC;BLUALL
FEDSEC;MEGA (cases)

Internet Sites

Eaton Vance Online: http://www.eatonvance.com

SEC News Digest—This Website analyzes the SEC's daily news digests, organizes all the material by subject matter, creates subject-specific News Digest Reports covering rule changes, recent 8K filings, Securities Act Registrations, and so on: http://www.jefren.com/sec/index.html.

ENDNOTES

1. David L. Ratner, *Securities in a Nutshell* (St. Paul, Minn.: West, 1992), 1.
2. Ibid., 2.
3. Ibid.
4. Ibid.
5. Ibid., 3.
6. Thomas Lee Hazen, *The Law of Securities Regulation* (St. Paul, Minn.: West, 1990), 3.
7. Ibid., 4.
8. Ibid.
9. Ibid.
10. Ibid.
11. Ibid.
12. Ibid.
13. Ibid.
14. Ibid.
15. Ibid., 5.
16. Ibid.
17. Ibid.
18. Ibid., 8.
19. Ibid.
20. Ibid., 8, 9.
21. Ibid., 11.
22. Ibid.

ASSIGNMENT A

Securities Research

Sources

Public library or Westlaw or Lexis for annual reports, 10Ks, and 10Qs
U.S.C.A.
Shepard's Acts and Cases by Popular Name
CCH Federal Securities Law Reporter
Robert Hamilton, *The Law of Corporations in a Nutshell*
Alan A. Palmiter, *Securities Regulation: Examples and Explanations*

A new software company, Computer Whiz, has recently gone public. The company, which was incorporated in 1996, is already a leader in maintaining and operating software for personal computers. The company is a privately held business; the CEO holds 48% of the stock.

1. Where would you find an annual report? (You can use Microsoft as an example.) What is the state of incorporation? (Hint: Westlaw: SEC-AR; or Lexis: COMPNY;ARS.)

2. Where would you find a 10K? What is the SIC code? (Hint: Westlaw: SEC-10K; or Lexis: COMPNY;10Q.)

3. Where would you find a 10Q? Who are the company's auditors? (Hint: Westlaw: SEC-10Q; or Lexis: COMPNY;10Q.)

4. Explain what a company has to do to go public. What does the Securities and Exchange Act of 1934 §15 say about reporting requirements? (Hint: A hornbook would be a good source.)

5. Find a 10K form by looking in the *Federal Securities Law Reporter*. Copy the form.

6. Look up 15 U.S.C.A. §78(c) and find what a penny stock is.

ASSIGNMENT B

Securities Research

Sources

Federal Securities Law Reporter
Thomas Lee Hazen, *The Law of Securities Regulation*
Robert Hamilton, *The Law of Corporations in a Nutshell*
Lexis
Westlaw

1. Where can you find the elements of Rule 10b-5? Cite a relevant case from the U.S. Supreme Court. (Hint: You can find the elements either in a hornbook or in a case.)

2. Rule 10b-5 is an anti-fraud provision, which was adopted by the SEC to prohibit "any manipulative or deceptive device or contrivance." The U.S. Supreme Court has held that no person can be found to have violated Rule 10b-5 unless he is shown to have acted with "scienter." Using the *Federal Securities Law Reporter*, find a case that discusses this scienter requirement. (Hint: You can also try Westlaw: FSEC-CS; or Lexis: FEDSEC;MEGA.)

3. Explain the Chinese Wall theory. Cite to the Merrill Lynch release involving the SEC. (Hint: Use a hornbook.)

4. Using the *Blue Sky Reporter*, find the Uniform Securities Act and find out whether fraud and deceit are limited to common law deceit.

CHAPTER 7

International Law

INTRODUCTION

International law (often called public international law) is generally defined as that body of rules or laws that regulates the interaction or relations among nations. Generally speaking, it is nations (called "states" in international law) that are the subject of international law rather than individuals, corporations, or other entities; however, this statement is becoming less true.

TREATIES AND DISPUTE SETTLEMENT

A treaty (convention, international agreement) is an international contract between states (countries).[1] A treaty between two states is bilateral; one between three or more states is multilateral. A state is bound in international law by the treaties to which it is a party, and it becomes a party by ratifying, approving, accepting, acceding, or adhering to the treaty pursuant to authority granted by the state's internal constitutional processes. For example, the United States becomes a party to a treaty after it has been signed by the President (or his representative), has received the advice on consent of the U.S. Senate, and has been ratified and proclaimed by the President.

A distinction is drawn in international law between the international legal obligations of a state that is a party to a treaty. States may participate in negotiations leading to the formation of a treaty and may, at the close of negotiations, sign the treaty without becoming bound fully in international law by the provisions of the treaty. The Vienna Convention (Article 18) takes the position that a signatory state to a treaty is obligated to refrain from acting in a way that would defeat the object and purpose of the treaty.

A state cannot invoke its internal law (including its Constitution) as an international legal justification for failing to perform its obligations under a treaty. However, courts within a state may disregard a relevant treaty in favor of applying some other treaty if the law of the state permits such a result. Nevertheless, such an action does not excuse the state from its international legal obligations.

Under Article 31 of the Vienna Convention, the terms of the treaty are to be given their ordinary meaning. As aids to interpretation, a court may use the treaty's text "including its preamble and annexes" and any other related agreement made between all the parties at the conclusion of the treaty and also any contemporaneous instrument accepted by the parties as related to the treaty.

THE INTERNATIONAL COURT OF JUSTICE

The International Court of Justice (ICJ) sits at The Hague, the Netherlands, and comprises fifteen judges drawn from all of the world's major legal systems. It is one of the principal organs of the United Nations (UN) and is the statutory, successor court to the former Permanent Court of International Justice of the League of Nations. The Statute of the ICJ limits the Court's jurisdiction and only allows states (countries) to be parties (have standing) before the Court in a contentious proceeding. The Court gives judgments in favor, or against, contesting states.

If a host country violates international law against an investor, for example, the state of which the investor is effectively a national may take up the grievance before the ICJ in a suit against the host country. However, an action before the ICJ is available only if the investor is complaining of official governmental conduct, not merely conduct by private parties and if the investor's own state seeks redress on the investor's behalf. The investor's state has complete discretion as to whether to espouse the claim and need not (except as its own law may provide) pay the investor any judgment proceeds awarded by the Court.

Article 36 of the Statute of the ICJ contains the Court's principal jurisdictional mandate and provides, in part, that the jurisdiction of the ICJ comprises all the cases that states refer to it and "all matters specially provided for" in treaties or in the UN Charter. States may recognize that the ICJ has compulsory jurisdiction on a reciprocal basis for interpretation of a treaty or a question of international law; whether a particular fact establishes a breach of an international obligation; and the appropriate remedy for any breach of an international obligation. Such recognition of compulsory jurisdiction may be made either unconditionally or conditioned upon the reciprocal recognition of ICJ jurisdictional by other states. ICJ judgments may include provisions for money damages and for injunctive relief and may be enforced by reference to the United Nations Security Council for further appropriate action, including military action, against a noncompliant party, according to Articles 39-51 and 94.2.

Article 38(1) of the ICJ Statute directs the ICJ to use international conventions, international custom, the general principles of law recognized by civilized nations, and judicial decisions of the various nations in deciding cases submitted to it.

HINT

Looking for international information? Try using the United Nations Treaty database on the Internet to find the information you need. The Website address is www.un.org/depts/treaty/.

BIBLIOGRAPHY

Loose-Leaf Services

Digest of Commercial Laws of the World. Dobbs Ferry, N.Y.: Oceana, 1998. This publication is a loose-leaf index of international commercial law. K7340.A49 1998.

Igor Kavass. *A Guide to the United States Treaties in Force*. Buffalo, N.Y.: William S. Hein, 1994. This is an index to U.S. treaties and agreements with access points by TIAS (Treaties and other International Acts Series) number, TS (U.S. Treaty Series) number, and other numbers. Includes indexing by subject and countries, and contains a chronological list of U.S. treaties and agreements. JX 236.5 T73 1994.

Treaties in Force: A List of Treaties and Other International Agreements of the U.S. Washington, D.C.: U.S. Department of State, 1956. This publication is a list of treaties and other international agreements of the United States in force since January 1, 1956; it is valuable as an index for U.S. treaties and for status checking of the treaties. JX 236.5 T7 1994.

United States Treaties and Other International Agreements (UST) (U.S. Treaty Series). Washington, D.C.: U.S. Department of State, 1950. UST publishes the official text of U.S. treaties and agreements from 1950; includes the text of each treaty in the language of each signatory. JX 236 1950.

Treatises

James R. Fox. *Dictionary of International & Comparative Law*. Dobbs Ferry, N.Y.: Oceana, 1992. This source not only explains legal terms, but also provides citations to many international treaties, agreements, and cases. JX 1226.F69, 1992.

Hornbooks

Ralph H. Folsom and Michael Wallace Gordon. *International Business Transactions*. St. Paul, Minn.: West, 1995 with 1996 pocket part.

Nutshells

Thomas Buergenthal and Harold G. Maier. *Public International Law in a Nutshell*. 2nd ed., St. Paul, Minn.: West, 1990.

Ralph H. Folsom, Michael Wallace Gordon, and John A. Spanogle Jr. *International Business Transactions in a Nutshell*. 5th ed. St. Paul, Minn.: West, 1996.

Atlases

National Geographic Atlas of the World. Washington, D.C.: National Geographic Society, 1999. G102.N38 1999.

Directories

Worldwide Government Directory with International Organizations. Washington, D.C.: Keesing's Worldwide, 1998. This directory is a gold mine of worldwide information about the governments of nations, worldwide, including information about the head of the government, government offices, and their telephone numbers. JF 37 .L345.

Statistical Sources

Statistical Abstract. New York: United Nations, 1999 (updated yearly). This publication includes statistics on culture, labor, agriculture, energy, transport, financial statistics, industry, manufacturing, and environment for each country of the world. HA 12.5.U63.

Statistical Yearbook. New York: United Nations, 1999. This publication has statistics on each country's energy, transportation, finances, industries, manufacturing, environment, and so on. HA 12.5 .U63.

Computer Sources

Westlaw

USTREATIES (U.S. Treaties & Other International Agreements)
IEL (International Economic Law)

Lexis

Library: (INTLAW)
Files: ILMTY (International Legal Materials); BDIEL (Basic Documents of International Economic Law); DSTATE (Department of State)
NAFTA (library); ILMTY (File) (North American Free Trade Agreement; Int'l Legal Materials)

Internet Sites

For EPA regulations, proposed rules, and environmental organizations, see http://www.EPA.gov.

ENDNOTES

1. This section and the next one are based on Ralph H. Folsom, *International Business Transactions* (St. Paul, Minn.: West, 1992).

ASSIGNMENT A

International Law Research

Sources

U.S. Treaties and Other International Agreements
Treaties in Force: A List of Treaties and Other International Agreements of the U.S. in Force on January 1, 1994
Digest of Commercial Laws of the World
Westlaw
Lexis

1. Look up *U.S. Treaties and Other International Agreements* in an electronic card catalog and find the catalog number. Then find the treaty between the United States and Pakistan concerning agricultural commodities. When was the treaty signed? In item IV, Export Limitations, what are the commodities to which limitations apply? Don't forget to cite your source.

2. Look up the catalog number and use *Treaties in Force: A List of Treaties and Other International Agreements of the U.S. in Force on January 1, 1994* (in the reference section). Give the following for the Commerce and Navigation Treaty with Turkey: Statutes at Large, cite, date of signature, TS number and date in force. In your answer, cite your source.

3. Look up in the card catalog and find the *Digest of Commercial Laws of the World*. In volume 2, look under Morocco Patent and Practice and find the two different kinds of patents in that country. Don't forget to cite your source.

4. Go on Lexis to find this English statute: Protection Trading Interests Act of 1980. Print the first page of the act. Use the INTLAW Library and UKCODE File.

5. Is there an agreement between the Dominican Republic and the United States concerning transfer of prisoners? Nothing is available in the law library or on the computers. What do you do? (Hint: Try the Embassy or Consulate's office in your state.)

ASSIGNMENT B

International Law Research

Sources

Digest of Commercial Laws of the World
Lexis
Westlaw

1. Is there a distinction between civil and commercial contracts in Peru?

2. Find a definition of Sharia law that is used in Omar and other Arab countries.

3. Find a treaty between the United States and Saudi Arabia discussing the air transport agreement between the two countries.

CHAPTER 8

Medical Research

INTRODUCTION

Medical research encompasses personal injury, medical malpractice, negligence, and products liability. Personal injury refers to injury to a person and is used in connection with negligence. One type of personal injury action is medical malpractice.

As early as 2000 B.C., the Code of Hammurabi evidenced concern for the quality of medical practice.[1] The Hippocratic Oath, written in the fourth century B.C., further defined standards for the medical profession.[2] Under English common law, physicians were regarded almost as members of a public calling, much the same as innkeepers, with their liability defined accordingly.[3] Later, the physician's role became a creation of contract law, with individual rights and liabilities established by the parties.[4] Tort principles have now largely dominated the law as the doctrine that defines professional medical liability.

The term *medical malpractice*, as used today, embraces all liability-producing conduct arising from the rendition of professional medical services.[5]

Today, medical malpractice law is a system of loss allocation that, for the most part, is based on the fault of the defendant. When a patient is injured by medical malpractice, the remedy he or she can pursue may be based on contract or tort, or both.[6] In the great majority of cases, the plaintiff alleges that the physician has in some way failed to perform in accordance with the required standard of care.[7] So, regardless of whether the physician–patient relationship is based on contract or tort, the duty of care is usually the same. Personal injury litigation has a preference of tort law.[8] In medical malpractice litigation, negligence is the predominant theory of liability.[9]

Negligence, according to the Restatement Second of Torts §282 (1965), has been defined as conduct that falls below the standard established by law for the protection of others against unreasonable risk of harm.[10]

To recover for negligent malpractice, the plaintiff must establish

1. that the physician owed a duty of care to the patient;
2. that the physician violated the applicable standard of care;
3. that the plaintiff suffered a compensable injury; and,
4. that such an injury was caused in fact and proximately by the substandard conduct.11 (The burden of proof is on the plaintiff.)

The formulation and nature of the standard of care has been articulated in *Blair v. Eblen*, 461 S.W.2d 370 (Ky. 1970):

> A physician is under a duty to use that degree of care and skill that is expected of a reasonably competent practitioner in the same class to which he belongs, acting in the same or similar circumstances.[12]

To establish the appropriate standard of care and a causal connection between the negligence and the injury, expert testimony is required.

In 1983, about 42,000 medical malpractice claims were filed in the United States.[13]

Personal injury also refers to actions of tort for negligence, which can include injuries from products (products liability), transportation accidents, injuries on your property or on the property of another, and injury to property or reputation. Actions under worker's compensation statutes are also included.[14]

Under the doctrine of strict products liability, a company that manufactures, designs, or sells a product may be legally responsible for injuries caused by the product. The injured person simply needs to show that the product was defective or had a defective design, or that there was a defective warning.[15]

Accidents involving no-fault insurance also fall under the category of personal injury. Under a no-fault system, a person involved in an accident is paid for losses from his or her own insurance company. If the person is partly responsible for the accident under contributory negligence rules, he or she cannot recover. Under comparative negligence, he or she can recover a portion of the damages if he or she were partially at fault.[16]

Companies that operate a bus, airplane, or train (common carriers) owe their passengers a high degree of care. Recovery for injuries depends on the circumstances surrounding the accident.

Defamation is also covered under personal injury.

GETTING STARTED

To begin medical research in any of these areas, get a definition of terms by looking at *Medical Terminology* by Love Smith. (See the sources in the bibliography following this section.) Other very basic tools are *Taber's Cyclopedic Medical Dictionary* or *Dorland's Illustrated Medical Dictionary*.

It is a good idea to familiarize yourself with the local medical library. Also, it never hurts to know a medical librarian who may be able to help you if the research gets especially difficult.

The *Directory of Medical Specialists* is invaluable if you need to know about the physician's certification or area of practice. Some basic textbooks include *Harrison's Principles of Internal Medicine, Robbins Pathologic Basis of Disease, Schwartz's Principles of Surgery, Andrew's Diseases of the Skin*, and the *Merke Manual of Diagnosis and Therapy*.

For questions regarding prescriptions and drugs, the *Physicians' Desk Reference for Prescription and Non-Prescription Drugs (PDR)* provides a wealth of information.

Periodical literature is found in the *Index Medicus*, or online in *Medline*, which is available free through the government, or through Lexis or Westlaw. Some of the other valuable databases include *Chem Abstracts, Index to Dental Literature, Cancerlit, Aidsline*, and *International Nursing Index*.

Some sources that give the legal point of view are the *Attorneys' Textbook of Medicine*, the *Lawyers' Guide to Medical Proof*, and *Proving Medical Diagnosis and Prognosis*.

HINTS

The prescription for success with medical research is to find a good medical library and check the books first. Second, *Medline* has proven to be an invaluable resource; it is available for free at many local public libraries on the Internet at http://medline.cos.com

BIBLIOGRAPHY

Beginning Your Medical Research

Genevieve Love Smith. *Medical Terminology*. 8th ed. Santa Barbara, Calif.: Delmar Publishing, 1999. (Programmed-learning text). This medical terminology text teaches a word-building system using a programmed-learning format that presents word parts and word building with over 1,700 frames. R123 .S6.

Dictionaries

Dorland's Illustrated Medical Dictionary. 28th ed. Philadelphia, Pa.: Saunders, 1994. This dictionary reflects new advances in medicine and current usage. Illustrations increase clarity and understanding. R123 .I57.

Stedman's Medical Dictionary. 26th ed. Philadelphia, Pa.: Lippincott, Williams, and Wilkins, 1995. In this medical dictionary, new terms have been added to reflect the growth of fields such as biotechnology, biochemistry, genetics, embryology, epidemiology, radiology, and neurology. Color illustrations highlight important definitions and provide a more exciting visual approach to medical language. R121 .S8 1995.

Clayton L. Thomas, ed. *Taber's Cyclopedic Medical Dictionary*. 18th ed. Philadelphia, Pa.: F.A. Davis, 1997. This is a comprehensive medical dictionary containing a broad spectrum of information that ranges from four-color illustrations to photomicrographs to detailed definitions. R121 .TI813 1997.

Basic Tools (Directories)

The Official ABMS Directory of Board Certified Medical Specialists. 31st ed. New Providence, N.J.: Marquis Who's Who, 1999 (updated yearly). This 4-volume set includes key information such as certification, medical school, year of degree, current academic appointments, academic titles, fellowships, and professional memberships, along with vital information such as name, address, and telephone number. R712 .Al .D5.

Basic Tools (Treatises)

Harry L. Arnold. *Andrew's Diseases of the Skin*. 8th ed. Philadelphia, Pa: W.B. Saunders, 1990. This is a comprehensive, illustrated book dealing with skin diseases. RL71 .A76 1990.

Henry Gray. *Gray's Anatomy*. 38th ed. London: Emery-Pratt, 1995. This reference has been acclaimed for its clear, lucid topographical descriptions and includes the latest cross-sectional imaging and extensive coverage of the anatomy encountered during endoscopic procedures. QM 23.2 .G73 1995.

Harrison's Principles of Internal Medicine. Gilford, Conn.: McGraw-Hill, 1998. This publication continues to define the practice of medicine into the next millennium. The comprehensive treatise examines the biologic and pathophysiologic origin of disease and charts a clear course for diagnosis and management. RC46 .H333 1998.

Merck Manual of Diagnosis and Therapy. 17th ed. San Diego, Calif.: Harcourt Brace, 1999. This manual contains current medical information used in the diagnosis and treatment process. Entries provide a definition or description of the illness or disease, etiology, symptoms and signs, diagnosis, prognosis, and treatment. RC55 .I48 1998.

Physicians' Desk Reference for Prescriptions Drugs. 53rd ed. Montvale, N.J.: Medical Economics Company, 1999; *Physicians' Desk Reference for Non-Prescription Drugs* 19th ed. Montvale, N.J.: Medical Economics Company, 1998. The *Physicians' Desk Reference for Prescriptions Drugs* provides usage information and warnings, drug interactions, plus more than 2,000 full-size, full-color photos cross-referenced to the drugs. This is the authoritative source of FDA-approved information on prescription drugs. The *Physicians' Desk Reference for Non-Prescription Drugs* offers full FDA-approved descriptions of the most commonly used over-the-counter (OTC) medicines. RC 81 .A2 P37 1999 and RM 671 .A1 .P48.

Seymour I. Schwartz, ed. *Principles of Surgery*. 7th ed. New York: McGraw-Hill, 1998. This publication includes the latest advances and techniques in transplantation, expanded coverage of surgical oncology, a new chapter on trauma, and a review of recent findings concerning systemic and metabolic response to injury. RD37.2 .S35.

Arnold G. Cogran, ed. *Robbins Pathologic Basis of Disease*. 6th ed. Philadelphia, Pa: W.B. Saunders, 1998. This edition carries on the tradition of excellence that has made its predecessors the gold standard: authoritative authorship, unparalleled readability, logical and consistent organization, and definitive, state-of-the-art coverage of every aspect of their specialty. R121 .TI813 1997.

Richard W. Rock. *TeLinde's Operative Gynecology*. 8th ed. Philadelphia, Pa: Lippincott, Williams, and Wilkins, 1997. This publication continues to offer a presentation that covers everything from the basics to the most current knowledge and techniques in gynecology. RG 104 .T4 1997.
Cunningham et al. *Williams Obstetrics.* 20th ed., Stanford, Conn.: Appleton and Lange, 1997. This book remains the premier source and the most thorough resource for the specialty of obstetrics. RG 524 .W7 1997.

Periodical Indexes

Cumulated Abridged Index Medicus. Washington, D.C.: U.S. Government Printing Office, 1995 (continuing annually until present). A cumulation of the *Abridged Index Medicus*. Z6660 .A51.
Index Medicus. Washington, D.C.: U.S. Government Printing Office, 1960 (continuing annually until present). The medical periodical literature index. Z6660 .I4

Computer Sources

Medline. 1966 to present. *Index Medicus* online (plus more journals) is available free through the National Library of Medicine or on Westlaw (through Dialog)(Medline) or Lexis (Medline).

Permuted Medical Subject Headings Index. National Technical Information Services (NTIS), 1993 (produced yearly), to be used as a thesaurus with *Medline.*

Westlaw

AIDSLINE (Westlaw/Dialog) 1980 forward +
BIOSIS (Westlaw through Dialog), 1969 + (Biotechnology and Life Sciences)
CANCERLIT (Westlaw/Dialog) 1963 +
CHEMENGABS (Chemical Engineering & Biotechnology Abstracts) 1971+
HSPHLTHSA (Hospital & Health Services Administration) 1994+
JAMDENTAL (Journal of the American Dental Association)
MRCKINDX (Merck Index On-Line: Drugs through Dialog/Westlaw) 19th Century+
CINAHL (Nursing and Allied Health through Dialog/Westlaw), 1983 +
PSYCINFO (through Dialog/Westlaw), 1887+

Also available (not on Lexis/Westlaw) are

CHEMICAL ABSTRACTS, available through Scientific and Technical Information Network
INDEX TO DENTAL LITERATURE, available through *Medline*, 1966+ and in hardcopy
INTERNATIONAL NURSING INDEX, available through *Medline*, 1966+ and in hardcopy

Lexis

NEWS/ASAPIN (Aids Alert) 1989+
HEALTH;ANDAID (Aids Litigation Reporter) 1996+
EMBASE;EMBASE (Worldwide Biomedicine & Pharmaceutical Research) 1974+
HEALTH;CTR (Cancer Treatment Reports) 1983–1987
ENVIRN;MSDS-T (Material Safety Data Sheets) OSHA Standards of Chemicals–Current
HEALTH;HOSP 1984+
HEALTH;DPF (Dental Practice Finance) 1966+
GENMED;DPF 1966+
GENMED;DIF (Drug Info Fulltext) current
GENMED;AHFS (American Hospital Formulary Service) current
BUSFIN;ABI (Nursing Management) current
NEWS;PSYTDY (Psychology Today) 1985+
GENMED;CURNWS (Journals and Newsletters) 1980s+

Sources That Give the Legal Point of View

Roscoe N. Gray. *Attorney's Textbook of Medicine.* 3rd ed. New York: Matthew Bender, 1992. This multivolume set with yearly updates has detailed, hard-to-find information on hundreds of injuries and disease, complete with diagnosis, treatment, prognosis, and medical-legal annotations. This text is written specifically for the practicing attorney. RA 1053 .G7 1992.

Lawyer's Guide to Medical Proof. 21st ed. New York: Matthew Bender, 1989. This multivolume loose-leaf with yearly updates provides practical, down-to-earth advice on the psychology of a personal injury trial, effective dramatic advocacy, and impeachment of expert witness testimony demonstrated by cross-examinations drawn from actual cases. This treatise clearly explains medical terminology, procedures, and technology and shows, through actual court records, how medical evidence can become an instrument of jury-convincing courtroom proof. KF8964 .H6.

Proving Medical Diagnosis and Prognosis. New York: Matthew Bender, 1985. This publication shows how hundreds of medical tests are performed and how to read their findings; it includes complete, authoritative guidance on orthopedic, neurological, laboratory, and other clinical tests and an in-depth discussion of medical records. RA 1053 .H6.

Internet Sources

Medline contains over 8,000,000 records from over 7,300 different medical and health-related publications: http://medline.cos.com.

ENDNOTES

1. Joseph H. King, *The Law of Medical Malpractice* (St. Paul, Minn.: West, 1986), 1.
2. Ibid.
3. Ibid., 2.
4. Ibid.
5. Ibid., 3.
6. Ibid., 6.
7. Ibid., 7.
8. Ibid.
9. Ibid., 9.
10. Ibid.
11. Ibid.
12. Ibid., 42.
13. *Encyclopedia Britannica Online*, Malpractice, p. 3, http://www.eb.com.
14. *Black's Law Dictionary* (St. Paul, Minn.: West, 1979), 707.
15. *Parson's Legal Information Network Online* (Available: http://www.go.com).
16. Ibid.

ASSIGNMENT A

Medical Research

Sources

Directory of Medical Specialists or *Official ABMS Directory of Board Certified Medical Specialists*
Dorland's Illustrated Medical Dictionary or *Taber's Cyclopedic Medical Dictionary*
Robbins Pathologic Basis of Disease
Index Medicus
Cumulated Abridged Index Medicus
Medline: Lexis: Medline; Medline
Westlaw: Medline
Internet: http://medline.cos.com/

1. Your boss at the law firm needs the name of a specialist on internal medicine who is from Pittsburgh, Pennsylvania. He also needs a definition or description of mesothelioma, a condition caused by prolonged exposure to asbestos. Find the article, "Malignant Mesothelioma and Duration of Asbestos Exposure: Correlation with Tissue Mineral Fiber Content," which appears in the *Annals of Occupational Hygiene*, volume 39, pp. 363–374, 1994 or 1995, and an article on largyngeal cancer and asbestos. (This is a hypothetical problem based on an actual problem.) Find the answers, plan a search strategy, and cite to your sources.

ASSIGNMENT B

Medical Research

Sources

Taber's Cyclopedic Medical Dictionary
Index Medicus
West's *Federal Practice Digest* or Genfed/Courts on Lexis or Allfeds on Westlaw

1. You are representing Lederle Laboratories, the defendant pharmaceutical company, against whom plaintiff, Libovitz, has brought suit. Libovitz was given Salk polio vaccine at 18 months and contracted polio. He is now an adult, age 22, and is in an iron lung. The issue deals with whether Lederle is liable under a negligence theory. Please familiarize yourself with the differences between Salk and Sabin vaccines. You also need to find cases and articles supporting Lederle's position. Because this is a diversity case, that is, the two parties are from different states, and the amount in controversy is over $75,000, you need to search for federal cases. Use federal digests in conjunction with Lexis, Westlaw, *Index Medicus*, and a medical dictionary. Plan a strategy.

ASSIGNMENT C

Medical Research

Sources

Robbins Pathologic Basis of Disease

1. Your supervising attorney has a picture of a diseased heart that has been damaged as a result of exposure to asbestos. She forgot where the picture came from. She has asked you to find the source. (Suggestions: Go to the medical library and find a book dealing with the basis of diseases.)

CHAPTER 9

Wills and Estates

INTRODUCTION

The statutes of all states prescribe certain formalities in the making and execution of wills. Except in certain cases, a will must be in writing; it may be handwritten (pen or pencil), typewritten, produced with word-processing equipment, or printed on virtually any type of material.[1]

A will may also be composed of separate documents.[2] An entirely separate document may become an integral part of a will under the doctrine of incorporation by reference.[3] The Uniform Probate Code, adopted in a number of jurisdictions, provides that any writing in existence when a will is executed may be incorporated by reference if the language of the will manifests this intent and describes the writing sufficiently to permit its identification.[4] Some states, however, have entirely rejected the doctrine of incorporation by reference, stating that an unattested paper that is of a testamentary nature cannot be taken as a part of a will even though referred to by that instrument.[5]

A will must be signed by the testator, although the signature may be by a mark.[6] The statutes of some states permit the signature to be written by a person other than the testator, so long as it is in the testator's presence and under his or her direction.[7] The laws of many states require that a will be signed at the end.[8] However, where the law of a state does not fix the location for the signature, it may be placed anywhere in the will.[9]

Attestation of a will consists of witnesses observing the act of the testator signing the will.[10] The number of witnesses differs in different states, but the Uniform Probate Code requires at least two witnesses.[11] Generally, it is required that the witnesses sign their names in the presence of the testator.[12]

The requirement that a will be published, which is imposed by statute in some states and not necessary in other states, is satisfied if the testator, by word or deed, clearly indicates to the witnesses that the instrument is a last will and testament.[13]

In some jurisdictions, other forms of wills are accepted as being able to pass property when a person dies. A holographic will is a will that is entirely written and signed by the testator in that person's own handwriting.[14]

A nuncupative will is a will that is not in writing and is declared by the testator as his or her will before witnesses.[15] Where allowed, an oral will can usually be made only when the testator is in a last illness and sometimes near death.[16] A joint will is a single instrument that contains the wills of two or more persons.[17] Mutual wills are those executed pursuant to an agreement between two or more persons to dispose of their property in a particular manner, each in consideration of the other.[18] Reciprocal wills are those in which the testators name each other as beneficiaries under similar testamentary plans.[19]

WHERE TO BEGIN

For an overview of the law of wills, begin by reading Thomas Atkinson's *Law of Wills.* (See the bibliography following this section for all references explained here.) Also refer to Robert Mennell's, *Wills and Trusts in a Nutshell.* Loose-leaf services such as the *BNA Pension and Benefits Reporter* or *CCH Pension Plan Guide* give comprehensive weekly reporting of the latest developments concerning estate planning. Some specialized treatises, such as *RIA Pension & Benefits Deskset,* deal with the full text of laws, committee reports, regulations, and finding aids.

Form books, such as Rabkin and Johnson's *Current Legal Forms with Tax Analysis,* deal with pension plans. Westlaw, Lexis, and the Internet have an abundance of material on wills, including forms, explanations, case law, rules, regulations, and legislative histories.

HINT

Cut your time in half—always check with your law firm first for forms. You can save yourself hours of work reinventing the wheel when there is already a form or sample on hand.

BIBLIOGRAPHY

Loose-Leaf Services

BNA Pension and Benefits Reporter. Washington, D.C.: Bureau of National Affairs, 1999. This is a comprehensive weekly reporting service of the latest developments influencing pensions and employee benefits and trust fund regulations. HD 7106.USB78a.

CCH COBRA Guide. Chicago, Ill.: Commerce Clearing House, 1999. This publication contains all the legal requirements of health care continuation coverage and insurance conversion rights. It explains complex rules and regulations that apply when COBRA coverage occurs because of an employee's death, divorce, legal separation, or reduction in work hours. KF 3605 .A6 .C65.

CCH Pension Plan Guide. Chicago, Ill.: Commerce Clearing House, 1999. This comprehensive loose-leaf service has everything the practitioner needs to set up, maintain, or revise a pension plan and to resolve day-to-day concerns. The publication has full-text coverage of ERISA and IRC regulations, releases, and rulings. KF 3512 .A6 .C65.

CCH Pensions and Deferred Compensation Guide. Chicago, Ill.: Commerce Clearing House, 1999. This is a quick-reference loose-leaf service for learning the essential steps for establishing and administering pension plans, with references to the IRC, ERISA, IRS, and DOL rulings. KF 3512.A6.p47.

RIA Estate Planners' Alert. Washington, D.C.: Research Institute of America, 1999. This monthly publication deals with critical developments in estate planning with highlights of the latest issues, trends, and techniques. KF 6571.A8 .E82.

Hornbooks

Thomas Atkinson, *Law of Wills*. St. Paul, Minn.: West, 1953. This is the classic comprehensive hornbook on estate and wills law that contains a treatment of all topics that may arise in the preparation or construction of wills. KF 753 .A98.

William McGovern, Sheldon Kurtz, and Jan Ellen Rein. *Wills, Trusts, and Estates—Including Taxation and Future Interests*. St. Paul, Minn.: West, 1988. This publication emphasizes the Uniform Probate Law. It introduces readers to the federal gift, estate, and generation skipping transfer tax laws and grantor trust rules affecting the wealth-distribution process. KF 755 .M34.

George T. Bogert. *Hornbook on Trusts*. 6th ed. St. Paul, Minn.: West, 1987. This publication covers topics discussing trusts. KF730.B64.1987.

Nutshells

Robert Lynn. *Introduction to Estate Planning in a Nutshell*. 4th ed. St. Paul, Minn.: West, 1992. This nutshell discusses wills, trusts, future interests, insurance, pension, federal estate, and gift taxation. KF 750 .L9.

Robert Mennell. *Wills and Trusts in a Nutshell.* St. Paul, Minn.: West, 1994. This nutshell is designed to supplement traditional coverage by pointing out particular areas of difficulty. KF 755 .Z9 .M38.

Lawrence H. Averill, Jr. *Uniform Probate Code in a Nutshell.* 4th ed. St. Paul, Minn.: West, 1996. This nutshell provides the student with a comprehensive explanation of the provisions and concepts of the code itself. KF765.Z95 A94 1996.

Annuals

Fundamental Concepts of Estate Administration. New York: Practicing Law Institute, 1999. This publication is an estate planning and administration course handbook. KF 6585 .F85.

Treatises

Michael G. Kushner. *ERISA: The Law and the Code.* Washington, D.C.: Bureau of National Affairs, 1998. This treatise alerts the practitioner to recent developments by highlighting new legislative material. In one volume, there is the full text of the Employee Retirement Income Security Act of 1974, relevant IRC provisions, and amendments. KF 3512.A315 G54 1998.

RIA Pension & Benefits Deskset. Washington, D.C.: Research Institute of America, 1999. This treatise has over 6,000 pages of full-text laws, committee reports, final and proposed regulations, and preambles, with finding aids in a 3-volume set. KF 3512.A329.

RIA Pension & Benefits Law. Washington, D.C.: Research Institute of America, 1999. This reference book features Congressional Committee Reports with tax, ERISA, and other statutory law. KF 3512 .A324 .P4

Forms

Jacob Rabkin and Mark H. Johnson. *Current Legal Forms with Tax Analysis.* New York: Matthew Bender, 1948 to present. This loose-leaf form book deals with partnerships, joint ventures, licenses, franchises, employment, and pension plans. KF 170.R3.

Computer Sources

Westlaw

BNA-TOC (Bureau of National Affairs Highlights and Contents)
PLI-EST (Practicing Law Institute Planning)
CCH-EGT (Commerce Clearing House Federal Estate and Gift Tax Reporter)
NYFORMSIDX-ESP (West's McKinney's Forms)

Lexis

ESTATE;WILLS (Will and Trust Forms)
BNA;PEN (BNA Pension & Benefits Reporter)
ESTATE;BENEF (RIA Employee Benefits Alert)
ESTATE;PLIEP (Practicing Law Institute Estate Planning)
ESTATE;MESP (Modern Estate Planning—Matthew Bender)

Internet Sites

The National Association of Estate Planning Attorney's Website offers question-and-answer databases on numerous estate planning topics; see http://www.healthquotes.net/cobra.htm and http://www.netplanning.com.

ENDNOTES

1. Thomas E. Atkinson, *Law of Wills* (St. Paul, Minn.: West, 1937), 6.
2. Ibid., 7.
3. Ibid.
4. Ibid.
5. Ibid.
6. Ibid.
7. Koran, Surah 4, An-Nisa.
8. Atkinson, 8.
9. Ibid., 9.
10. Ibid.
11. Ibid., 11.
12. Ibid., 13.
13. Ibid., 18, 19.
14. Ibid., 22.
15. Ibid., 28.
16. Ibid., 33.
17. Ibid., 36.
18. Ibid.
19. Ibid.

ASSIGNMENT A

Wills and Estates Research

Sources

CCH Pension Plan Guide
CCH COBRA Guide
Internet: http://www.healthquotes.net/cobra.htm
Rabkin and Johnson, *Current Legal Forms with Tax Analysis*

1. Using Rabkin and Johnson, *Current Legal Forms with Tax Analysis*, Volume 10, Chapter 7, find an Estate Planning Devices checklist. On which page is the checklist located? Photocopy the first page.

2. Now find a checklist for Pension Plans in the *CCH Pension Plan Guide*. Look in the topical index under "normal retirement benefits" and find out when a participant will be eligible for an early retirement.

3. Explain in detail what COBRA means. To find a definition and explanation of COBRA, search "COBRA health" at http://www.healthquotes.net/cobra.htm.

4. Now look in the *CCH COBRA Guide, Cumulative Index*. Does a spouse dropped from a COBRA plan before a divorce have COBRA rights? Cite the IRS proposed regulation on this section.

5. Look in the *Florida Probate Code Manual* by David T. Smith and find a model will.

ASSIGNMENT B

Wills and Estates Research

Sources

Lexis
Westlaw
Atkinson, *Law of Wills,* or another hornbook

1. Find the general requirements for "testamentary capacity" by looking in Atkinson, *Law of Wills*. Does extreme old age disqualify one from making a will?

2. Search on Lexis in the Estate Library and in the Modern Estate Planning file by Matthew Bender: ESTATE;MESP. (You can also try a similar search on Westlaw.) Find out what is the basic format (the basic formalities) for drafting a durable power of attorney for property management. There is an entry dealing with the Elderly Client and Planning for Incapacity.

3. Using Westlaw, *West's McKinney's Forms*, NYYFORMSIDX-ESP, find a form for a testamentary capacity, particularly one that deals with "Dismissing Probate of the Will on the Basis of Lack of Testamentary Capacity." Cite to, and copy, one of the forms. (Hint: Remember, on Westlaw, if you want to search for testamentary before capacity, you should search "testamentary +3 capacity.") You can also try the search on Lexis: "testamentary pre/3 capacity."

4. Using either Westlaw or Lexis, find the *Merrick v. Continental Illinois National Bank* case dealing with testamentary capacity and the elderly. On Westlaw, you can search MEPP-CS (Multistate Estate Planning and Probate Cases) or ALLSTATES. You can also try the search in Lexis: ESTATE;PENS or another library and file. Cite the case and explain the holding.

Model Wills

1. Spouse—All Will

LAST WILL

OF

1, ________ ________ ________ also known as ________ ________ ________ domiciled and residing in the City of ______________ ______________ County, Florida, declare this to be my LAST WILL, and hereby revoke all prior wills and codicils to them.

ITEM I

All property which I own or of which I have the rights of disposal at my death, I give to my beloved wife, ________ ________ ________ also known as ________ absolutely and in fee simple. I make no provision for any children I may now have, and specifically disinherit any child or children born or adopted by me hereafter, having full faith and trust that my wife will adequately provide for them.

ITEM II

Should, however, my wife, ________ ________ ________, fail to survive me by thirty days, then ITEM I shall fail and be of no effect; and in that event, all property which I own or of which I have rights of disposal at my death, I give in equal share to such of my children as survive me, absolutely and in fee simple. Should any of my children fail to survive me, leaving issue surviving, such issue shall take the deceased child's share, per stirpes.

ITEM III

As used herein, the terms child, children, and issue include persons born in wedlock and adopted persons.

ITEM IV

In the event my wife, ________ ________ ________, should predecease me, I appoint my brother, ________ ________ ________ presently residing in the City of ________ ________, County, Florida as GUARDIAN of the person and ________ property of any child or children who may at the time be minors.

ITEM V

I appoint my wife, ________ ________ ________, as PERSONAL REPRESENTATIVE of my estate and direct that she serve without bond. In addition to the powers conferred upon personal representatives by law, she shall have full power, in her discretion and without any court order or proceeding to lease, or to sell pursuant to option or otherwise at public or private sale and upon such terms as she shall deem best, any real or personal property belonging to my estate, without regard to the necessity of such sale for the purpose of paying debts, taxes or devises; or to retain any or all of such property not so required, without liability for any depreciation thereof; to make distribution in kind; to assign or transfer certificates of stock, bonds or other securities; to adjust, compromise and settle all matters of business and claims in favor of or against my estate; to continue any unincorporated business for the period of administration, or to incorporate any business in which I may be engaged at the time of my death and to continue that incorporated business throughout the period of administration; and to do any and all things necessary or proper to complete the administration of my estate, all as fully as I could do myself.

In the event my wife, ________ ________ ________, should predecease me, or for any reason fails to qualify as PERSONAL REPRESENTATIVE of this will, or having qualified, thereafter for any reason shall cease to act, then I appoint my brother, ________ ________ ________ presently residing in the City of ________ ________ County, Florida as PERSONAL REPRESENTATIVE of this will and direct that he serve without bond. He is to have all the duties, rights, powers, liabilities, privileges and immunities which are hereinbefore given to my said wife, ________ ________ ________ as PERSONAL REPRESENTATIVE as aforesaid. IN WITNESS WHEREOF, I have on this ________ day of ________ 20__, at ________, Florida, declared this instrument of ________ pages to be my will and now sign this will, in the presence of the witnesses whose names appear below, and request that they witness my signature and attest to the execution of this will.

____

(Name of Testator)

On ________ ________, 20__ the foregoing instrument was signed by the said ________ ________ in our presence and was by him declared to be his LAST WILL, and we at this request, in his presence, and in the presence of each other, have hereunto subscribed our names as attesting witnesses.

________________________________ residing at ________________________________

________________________________ residing at ________________________________

________________________________ residing at ________________________________

2. Husband's Pour Over Will to Trust Agreement

LAST WILL

OF

I, ________ ________ ________ also known as ________ ________ ________ domiciled and residing in the City of ________ ________ County, Florida, declare this to be my LAST WILL, and hereby revoke all prior wills and codicils to them.

ITEM I

I devise all of my non-business tangible personal property to my wife, ________________, also known as ________________, absolutely, if she shall survive me, but if she shall not survive me, in equal shares to such of my children as shall survive me, to be divided among them as they may agree, or if they are unable to agree, as my PERSONAL REPRESENTATIVE shall decide. I devise to my wife, ________________, if she shall survive me, all of my right, title and interest in and to any residence or residences that I may be using at the time of my death, subject, however, to any mortgage encumbrance thereon.

ITEM II

All of the rest and remainder of my property, I devise to ________________ Bank of ________ Florida, TRUSTEE, in augmentation of the property held by it under the terms of a certain TRUST AGREEMENT entered into this date between me and said bank, as the same may be hereafter amended in writing. If necessary to give effect to this item, but not otherwise, the

provisions of said TRUST AGREEMENT are hereby incorporated by reference as fully as though restated herein, and I direct that no bond be required of said TRUSTEE.
If, at the time for my PERSONAL REPRESENTATIVE to make distribution to the TRUSTEE under my aforementioned TRUST AGREEMENT, any trust beneficiary is then entitled to distribution of trust assets from the TRUSTEE, my PERSONAL REPRESENTATIVE may make distribution directly to such beneficiary.

ITEM III

I appoint _______________ Bank of _______________, Florida, as PERSONAL REPRESENTATIVE of my estate and direct that it serve without bond. In addition to the powers conferred upon personal representatives by law, my PERSONAL REPRESENTATIVE shall have the following powers:

(a) to sell or exchange, at public or private sale and on credit or otherwise, to grant options to buy and to lease for any term, or perpetually, any property constituting a part of my probate estate; to invest and reinvest in, and to retain, whether originally a part of my estate or subsequently acquired, real or personal property of every kind and description (including stock or other securities of ________ Bank) without being subject to any investment or diversification restrictions, statutory or judicial, whenever prescribed;

(b) to represent and vote or to issue proxies, with powers of substitution, for stocks, bonds or other securities; to enter into or oppose any plan of merger, liquidation, lease, sale, mortgage, consolidation, reorganization or foreclosure, and, in connection therewith to pay amounts due under such plan, deposit securities and delegate discretionary powers to an agent or protective committee; and to exercise, buy or sell rights of conversion or subscription;

(c) to compromise, settle, release or adjust all matters of business and claims in favor of or against my estate;

(d) to make divisions or distributions of property in kind or in money or partly in each;

(e) to execute and deliver all necessary or proper deeds or other instruments;

(f) to continue any unincorporated business for the period of administration, or to incorporate any business in which I may be engaged at the time of my death and to continue that incorporated business throughout the period of administration, without court order and without liability for losses;

(g) when a choice is available as to whether certain deductions shall be taken as income tax deductions or as estate tax deductions, the decision of my PERSONAL REPRESENTATIVE in this regard shall be conclusive on all concerned and no adjustment of the income and principal accounts of my estate shall be made as the result of such decision; without duty to give or obtain consideration therefor, to join with my wife or her estate in the filing of any federal income tax returns for any year for which I have not filed such return prior to my death; to consent to any gifts made by her as being made half by me for the purpose of the federal gift tax law; and to take such action even though it may result in additional liabilities for my estate. Any income or gift taxes due on such returns, and any deficiencies, interest or penalties thereon, shall be allocated in such manner between my estate and my wife or her estate or all to any of them, as my PERSONAL REPRESENTATIVE shall deem proper;

(i) to borrow money, at interest, from itself or from others, for the benefit of my estate, and to pledge or mortgage property of the estate as security therefor; and to do any and all things necessary or proper to complete the administration of my estate, all as fully as I could do myself.

Anything herein to the contrary notwithstanding, with respect to any close corporation shares constituting a part of my probate estate, my PERSONAL REPRESENTATIVE shall vote, exchange and/or sell the same only upon the direction of the acting advisor, hereinafter named, to be confirmed in writing. Further, my PERSONAL REPRESENTATIVE shall make no leases, sales, exchanges, or investments of other assets constituting a part of my probate estate except with the approval of the acting advisor, to be confirmed in writing. My PERSONAL REPRESENTATIVE shall not be liable for any loss resulting from complying with the directions of such advisor nor from the retention of any asset, the sale, lease, or exchange of which it has proposed but which sale, lease, or exchange the advisor has failed to approve. My PERSONAL REPRESENTATIVE shall have no duty while an advisor is serving hereunder to make any investment review or recommendation with respect to shares of any close corporation constituting a part of my probate estate, any statute, rule of law or regulation to the contrary notwithstanding. No person dealing with my PERSONAL REPRESENTATIVE shall be under any obligation to ascertain whether such direction or approval has been obtained. I designate as advisor hereunder the following persons, to serve successively and in the order named: ______________________

If there be no advisor willing and able, in the opinion of my PERSONAL REPRESENTATIVE, to serve as provided herein, my PERSONAL REPRESENTATIVE shall exercise its sole discretion in such matters.

My PERSONAL REPRESENTATIVE shall pay from the property disposed of in ITEM II all inheritance, estate and other death taxes arising by reason of my death, including interest and penalties. No payment shall be made of a generation-skipping tax. My PERSONAL REPRESENTATIVE shall have no power to seek contribution or reimbursement therefor from any person or property, except from the TRUSTEE referred to above, which is authorized to supply funds to my PERSONAL REPRESENTATIVE to pay such death taxes, interest and penalties.

IN WITNESS WHEREOF, I have on this _______ day of _______, 20__, at _______, Florida, declared this instrument of _______ pages to be my will and now sign this will, in the presence of the witnesses whose names appear below, and request that they witness my signature and attest to the execution of this will.

(Name of Testator)

On _______ _______, 20__ the foregoing instrument was Signed by the _______ _______ in our presence and was by him declared to be his LAST WILL, and we at his request, in his presence, and in the presence of each other, have hereunto subscribed our names as attesting witnesses.

______________________________ residing at ______________________________

______________________________ residing at ______________________________

______________________________ residing at ______________________________

3. Wife's Pour Over Will to Husband's Trust

LAST WILL

OF

I, ________ ________ ________, also known as ________ ________ ________ domiciled and residing in the City of ________ ________ County, Florida, declare this to be my LAST WILL, and hereby revoke all prior wills and codicils to them.

ITEM I

I devise all of my tangible personal property to my husband, ________________, also known as ________________, absolutely, if he shall survive me, but if he shall not survive me, in equal shares to such of my children as shall survive me, to be divided among them as they may agree, or if they are unable to agree, as my PERSONAL REPRESENTATIVE shall decide.

ITEM II

All of the rest and remainder of my property, I devise to my husband ________ ________ ________, if he shall survive me by at least six (6) months, but if he shall not survive me by such period of time, then to ________ Bank of ________, Florida. TRUSTEE, in augmentation of the property then held or to be held under the terms of a certain TRUST AGREEMENT heretofore entered into between my husband and said bank dated ________ ________, for disposition in accordance with the provisions of such agreement, including any written modification thereof made prior to my death; provided, however, that if at the time for my PERSONAL REPRESENTATIVE to make distribution to the TRUSTEE under said TRUST AGREEMENT any trust beneficiary is then entitled to distribution of trust assets from the TRUSTEE, my PERSONAL REPRESENTATIVE may make distribution directly to such beneficiary. If necessary to give effect to this item, but not otherwise, the provisions of said TRUST AGREEMENT are hereby incorporated by reference as fully as though restated herein, and I direct that no bond be required of said TRUSTEE.

If I shall survive my husband, I specifically exercise in favor of my estate the power of appointment referred to in Article ________ of said TRUST AGREEMENT established by my husband, identified above, in an amount equal to all death taxes arising by reason of my death, including interest and penalties, and my PERSONAL REPRESENTATIVE is accordingly directed to obtain funds from said TRUSTEE. Except to the extent provided for in this paragraph, I specifically decline to exercise the power of appointment referred to herein.

ITEM III

I appoint my husband, ________________ as PERSONAL REPRESENTATIVE of my estate, but if my husband shall fail to qualify as PERSONAL REPRESENTATIVE hereunder or having qualified shall fail to complete the administration of my estate, then I appoint ________ Bank of ________ Florida, as PERSONAL REPRESENTATIVE in my husband's place and stead with the same powers, duties and immunities. No bond shall be required of any PERSONAL REPRESENTATIVE named herein. In addition to the powers conferred upon personal representatives by law, my PERSONAL REPRESENTATIVE shall have the following powers:

(a) to sell or exchange, at public or private sale and on credit or otherwise, to grant options to buy and to lease for any term, or perpetually, any property constituting a part of my probate estate; to invest and reinvest in, and to retain, whether originally a part of my estate or subsequently acquired, real or personal property of every kind and description (including stock or other securities of ________ Bank) without being subject to any investment or diversification restrictions, statutory or judicial, whenever prescribed;

(b) to represent and vote or to issue proxies, with powers of substitution, for stocks, bonds or other securities; to enter into or oppose any plan of merger, liquidation, lease, sale, mortgage, consolidation, reorganization, or foreclosure, and, in connection therewith to pay amounts due under such plan, deposit securities and delegate discretionary powers to an agent or protective committee; and to exercise, buy or sell rights of conversion or subscription;

(c) to compromise, settle, release or adjust all matters of business and claims in favor of or against my estate;

(d) to make divisions or distributions of property in kind or in money or partly in each;

(e) to execute and deliver all necessary or proper deeds or other instruments;

(f) to continue any unincorporated business for the period of administration, or to incorporate any business in which I may be engaged at the time of my death and to continue that incorporated business throughout the period of administration, without court order and without liability for losses;

(g) when a choice is available as to whether certain deductions shall be taken as income tax deductions or as estate tax deductions, the decision of my PERSONAL REPRESENTATIVE in this regard shall be conclusive on all concerned and no adjustment of the income and principal accounts of my estate shall be made as the result of such decision;

(h) without duty to give or obtain consideration therefor, to join with my husband or his estate in the filing of any federal income tax returns for any year for which I have not filed such return prior to my death; to consent to any gifts made by him as being made half by me for the purpose of the federal gift tax law; and to take such action even though it may result in additional liabilities for my estate. Any income or gift taxes due on such returns, and any deficiencies, interest or penalties thereon, shall be allocated in such manner between my estate and my husband or his estate or all to any of them, as my PERSONAL REPRESENTATIVE shall deem proper;

(i) to borrow money, at interest, from itself or from others, for the benefit of my estate, and to pledge or mortgage property of the estate as security there for;

and to do any and all things necessary or proper to complete the administration of my estate, all as fully as I could do myself.

My PERSONAL REPRESENTATIVE shall pay from the property disposed of in ITEM II all inheritance, estate, and other death taxes arising by reason of my death including interest and penalties, and shall have no power to seek contribution or reimbursement from any person or property therefor.

IN WITNESS WHEREOF, I have on this _______ day of _______, 20__, at _______, Florida, declared this instrument of _______ pages to be my will and now sign this will, in the presence of the witnesses whose names appear below, and request that they witness my signature and attest to the execution of this will.

____

(Name of Testatrix)

On _______ _______, 20__ the foregoing instrument was signed by the said _______ _______ _______ in our presence and was by her declared to be her LAST WILL, and we at her request, in her presence, and in the presence of each other, have hereunto subscribed our names as attesting witnesses.

______________________________ residing at ______________________________

______________________________ residing at ______________________________

______________________________ residing at ______________________________

CHAPTER 10

Government Publications/Legislative History

INTRODUCTION

A legislative history is not a history in the usual sense of a narrative record or interpretation of past events.[1] Rather, a legislative history is research into the drafting of a statute. The purpose of a legislative history is to clear up the ambiguity of statutory language, to persuade the court to accept a given interpretation, and to gather information with which to work.

THE LEGISLATIVE PROCESS

Legislation first starts out as a bill. After the bill is proposed, it goes to the House. The bill is then sent to a committee, which sends the bill to subcommittee. Or, the committee may decide to sponsor a special study to be done. Drafts from the committees are called Committee Prints. Many times, the bill is proposed in a given form or it is rewritten. The bill then comes out of the committee as a Committee Report. It goes to the floor of the House of Representatives, where it can vote on or amend the bill. Then the bill goes to the other chamber of representatives, the Senate. A Senate committee may report the bill or change it. The bill becomes a law when it goes to the President, who has thirty days to sign it or veto it. If the President does not approve the bill, it can still become a law if approved by two-thirds of the House or Senate (an override vote). Then the bill still becomes a law even if the President disapproves.

American statutes are then published as slip laws (the official text of the law in one page or in a pamphlet). Next are the session laws, which are published in the Statutes at Large in separate volumes for each year, or session, of the legislature. Then the session laws become public laws, and finally codes, which are published in the U.S. Code.

The object of a legislative history is to find the intent of the bill. There are three main sources for legislative histories:

1. The *Monthly Catalog*, published by the Government Printing Office (GPO) since 1895, is a cumbersome tool that is difficult to use because it is not indexed well. It is the main source for what the government publishes, and it provides the Superintendent of Documents classification numbers used to shelve documents in most libraries.[2] *The Monthly Catalog* can be searched online through the Dialog computer system.[3]

2. The *Congressional Information Service (CIS)* has coverage of bills, hearings, committee reports, debates, committee prints, House and Senate documents, Presidential documents, and all legislative actions. Coverage runs from 1970 until the present. There are index and abstracts volumes, along with legislative history volumes. CIS has indexes by subject, title, bill number, report number, and hearing number. Organization is great.

3. The *United States Code, Congressional, and Administrative News (USCCAN)*, published by West, has coverage from 1944 on. *USCCAN* is an advance session law service for federal statutes; it not only publishes the text of statutes, but also has selective legislative materials leading to their enactment, such as House and Senate reports.[4]

OTHER USEFUL TOOLS

The *Congressional Record*, where the floor debate is published, is a publication of the public proceedings of Congress. First published in 1873, the *Congressional Record* has predecessors back to 1789. It is published every day that the Congress is in session. The *Congressional Record* contains a transcript of the proceedings from the floors of the House and Senate.

The *Daily Digest* is a summary of bills and resolutions introduced, bills and resolutions reported out of committee, measures passed, and nominations confirmed. It tells when meetings are scheduled. The first issue of the month is a resumé congressional action.

Federal information on the status of bills–both House and Senate–can be obtained by calling the House of Senate Documents Room in Washington, D.C., at (202)225-1772 (House) or (202)224-2120 (Senate). Both of these offices can give the status of a bill and the action that has been taken on the legislation. Photocopied pages are available for $0.50 a page.

STATE LEGISLATIVE HISTORIES

As far as state legislative histories go, the only thing available in many cases is the debate, which is published in the state House and Senate Legislative Journals. Information on state legislative histories is difficult to find. For most state information regarding legislative histories, information can be found by calling the state county law library in the capitol or by trying a large law school that has a government depository.

HINT

For federal information on the status of bills, save time by calling the House Documents Room in Washington, D.C., at (202) 225-1772 or the Senate Documents Room at (202) 224-2120.

BIBLIOGRAPHY

Directories

The Code of Federal Regulations. Washington, D.C.: U.S. Government Printing Office, 1999. First published in 1937, and then annually since 1949, this publication is the codification of the Federal Register. It's a useful analogy to compare the *Code of Federal Regulations (CFR)* to the United States Code (USC). Just as the Statutes at Large are codified in the USC, so are the daily issues of the Federal Register codified in the *CFR*. The *CFR* is revised and published at least once a year at quarterly intervals. AE 2.106/3:40.

The Federal Register. Washington, D.C.: U.S. Government Printing Office, 1999. This publication has been issued Monday through Friday since 1936–five days a week except on official holidays. It contains regulations, proposed regulations, presidential proclamations and executive orders, background analyses regarding agency actions, hearings, grants, and publications. The *Federal Register* updates the Code of Federal Regulations. AE 2.106/3:40.

The Congressional Yellow Book. New York: Leadership Directories, 1999. This loose-leaf directory is issued quarterly and contains directory-type information on members of Congress, their committees, and key staff aides. Also included are key personnel of the Library of Congress, the Government Printing Office, and the General Accounting Office. JK 1010 .C68.

The Federal Yellow Book. New York: Leadership Directories, 1999. Like its counterpart for Capitol Hill (the *Official Congressional Directory*), this loose-leaf locator directory covers the White House, Executive Office of the President, and the federal departments and agencies. It lists federal employees by organizations with their names, titles, addresses, rooms, and telephone numbers. The directory is kept current with replacement pages issued irregularly several times a year. JK 6 .F45.

The Official Congressional Directory. New York: Leadership Directories, 1999. Issued for each session, this directory gives organizational and personnel information for executive, legislative, and judicial branches, with emphasis on Congress. It also gives biographies of members of Congress, information on committees, data on others associated with Congress, information on diplomats, and international organizations. Y4.P 93/1:1/

The U.S. Government Manual. Washington, D.C.: U.S. Government Printing Office, 1999. This is the official handbook of the federal government, describing the purposes and programs of most governmental agencies. This annual publication gives the names of chief personnel as well as excellent information about the programs and activities of the legislative, judicial, and executive branches. JK 421 .A3.

Legislative Information

The Congressional Record. Washington, D.C.: U.S. Government Printing Office, 1999. This is a verbatim record of the activities of Congress on the floors of the House and Senate. The *Congressional Record (CR)* is issued daily, and later these daily volumes are cumulated into bound volumes. A separate biweekly index provides access by names and subjects and a History of Bills and Resolutions. This separate index is the most useful for following the legislative process, because references are given to pages of the *Congressional Record* that have action on a particular bill. Because this section is cumulative, only the latest issue of the index needs to be consulted. The final bound volumes also have an annual separate index. This index includes a Daily Digest section, containing a chronological summary of actions, a name and subject index, and the History of Bills and Resolutions index. X 1.1/a:V/N.

The House and Senate Journals. Washington, D.C.: U.S. Government Printing Office, 1999. These journals are published annually at the end of a session. They are not verbatim, but cover each House's actions, votes, procedures, motions, and so on. XJH: 103-1/pt. 1-2.

Published Congressional Materials–Bills and Resolutions

Bills are commonly used to pass legislation; resolutions are commonly used for passing matters concerning only one House. Concurrent resolutions are used for matters affecting the operation of both houses. All of these are available through the depository system on microfiche. If the material is very current, you can call the House or Senate Documents Rooms:

House: (202) 225-3456
Senate: (202) 224-2971

For the status of bills, call (202) 225-1972. (Bills can be sent to you for $0.50 per page.)

Published Congressional Materials–Reports and Documents

House and Senate reports are issued by the individual Congressional committees and are available by calling the sponsoring legislator. Reports may also be issued as "conference reports," which reconcile differences in similar legislation passed by the House and Senate. These are also available through the House and Senate Document Rooms or the Government Printing Office.

House and Senate documents include texts of presidential messages or special reports submitted to Congress. They are first issued individually and then issued into a Serial Set. From the 97th Congress on, the *Monthly Catalog* includes a listing of individual reports.

Hearings and Committee Reports

Hearings and committee reports are assigned Superintendent of Documents numbers beginning with Y4 and are available in the *Monthly Catalog*.

Statutory Material

Laws are first issued as individual documents, called slip laws. These individual slip laws are later bound chronologically into the Statutes at Large. All current laws are also arranged by subject into titles and republished in the U.S. Code. The U.S. Code is composed only of those laws that are currently in effect.

Sources for Researching a Legislative History

Congressional Information Service (CIS), Washington, D.C., is an excellent commercial publisher. CIS began in 1970 and covers nearly all congressional publications, except for the *Congressional Record*. This service indexes hearings, reports, prints, and documents by subject, title, name, number, and sponsor. CIS is published monthly, with quarterly cumulations and annual volumes. The annual volumes include comprehensive legislative histories, with references to bills, hearings, reports, debates, presidential documents, and all legislative actions. There are both abstract volumes and legislative history volumes. CIS offers microfiche files of bills and laws that are probably the most complete in existence.

The Monthly Catalog of Government Publications. Washington, D.C.: U.S. Government Printing Office, 1999. This is the U.S. government's rendition of the CIS. A cumbersome, but extensive tool, the *Monthly Catalog* has coverage from the 1700s to the present. Many of the materials are on microfiche and are hard to copy.

United States Code, Congressional, and Administrative News (USCCAN). St. Paul, Minn.: West, 1944 to present. This publication first appears in a monthly advance sheet and is then compiled in bound volumes at the end of each Congressional session. *USCCAN*, the companion to the *USCA*, contains the complete text of all public laws and selected reprints of Congressional committee reports. It also includes selected administrative regulations, executive documents, amendments to court rules, and tables and indexes to other publications.

Nutshell

Jack Davies. *Legislative Law and Process in a Nutshell*. 2nd ed. St. Paul, Minn.: West, 1986.

Hornbook

William P. Statsky. *Legislative Analysis and Drafting*. 2nd ed. St. Paul, Minn.: West, 1984.

Computer Sources

Westlaw

FR (Federal Register)
CFR (Code of Federal Regulations)
LH (Legislative History)
LEGIS-ALL-MULTISTATE (legislative materials)
BNA-TRCK
CIS (Congressional Information Service)

Lexis

GENFED;CFR (Code of Federal Regulations)
GENFED;FEDREG
LEGIS;BILLS (legislative materials)
GENFED;BLTRCK (bill tracking)

Internet

Thomas is the U.S. Congress on the Internet; this home page has current U.S. federal legislative information, including bills, laws, the Congressional Record, reports, and links to further information: http://thomas.loc.gov/.

Legislative histories can be found through the Superintendent of Documents home page at http://www.access.gpo.gov/su_docs.

ENDNOTES

1. Morris L. Cohen and Robert C. Berring, *Finding the Law* (St. Paul, Minn.: West, 1989).
2. Ibid., 297.
3. Ibid.
4. Ibid., 149.

ASSIGNMENT A

Government Documents/Legislative Histories

Sources

Federal Yellow Book
Congressional Yellow Book
Congressional Staff Directory
Statistical Abstract of the United States
Vital Statistics of the United States
U.S. Government Manual

1. Use the *Federal Yellow Book* to find, under the Smithsonian Institution, the name and telephone number of the General Counsel.

2. Locate the *Congressional Yellow Book* and list the senators in your state, their date of reelection, profession, and date of birth.

3. Use the *Congressional Staff Directory* to find Representative Anna G. Eshoo's address, telephone number, and the state she represents. (This information can also be found at http://thomas.loc.gov/.)

4. Use the *Statistical Abstract of the United States* to find the foreign exchange rate of the Hong Kong dollar to the U.S. dollar. (You can also use http://www.census.gov.)

5. Use *Vital Statistics of the United States* (table) to find out how many deaths were by complication of pregnancy and childbirth in Texas in 1998.

6. Locate the *U.S. Government Manual*. Who is the Secretary of Housing and Urban Development (HUD)? What is the address and phone number of HUD? What is the date of the edition you used and the page number? (You can also use http://www.access.gpo.gov/nara/nara001.html.)

ASSIGNMENT B

Government Documents/Legislative Histories

Sources

Congressional Information Service (CIS)
U.S. Code, Congressional, and Administrative News (USCCAN)

1. Use the 1975-78 *CIS* Cumulative Index and find the abstract number (77-_____-11) for the Federal Election Campaign Act Amendments of 1974.

2. Using the abstracts volume (CIS/annual 1977) of the *Congressional Information Service*, find the abstract on the Federal Election Campaign Act Amendments of 1974.

3. What do these amendments recommend and amend?

4. What is the Senate Report Number?

5. What is the date of approval?

6. What does Part 2 reduce?

7. Look up Public Law (PL 93-443) in *USCCAN* (93rd Congress, vol. 3, Legislative History). List two of the eight principles of the act (p. 5589).

8. Are minor parties eligible to receive a fair share of public assistance? (p. 5594).

9. Search on Netscape, Microsoft Internet Explorer, or another Internet browser for http://thomas.loc.gov. Type in copyright and look up H.R. 320. What does this House Resolution deal with?

10. Who is the sponsor?

CHAPTER 11

Environmental Law

INTRODUCTION

During the years from 1776 until 1860 in the United States, three things dominated U.S. law and politics: the development of natural resources, the creation of a national economy, and slavery.[1] Primacy of land was a major issue, particularly among Southern congressmen, who exercised strong controls, demanding that land be managed so as not to threaten the institution of slavery.

Between 1780 and 1803, the states ceded 541 million acres to the national government. The creation of public lands was the first step in establishing an environmental commons, or national park system. Many point to the U.S. national park system as one of our country's great achievements, and Yellowstone's creation was celebrated by environmentalists around the world.

Following the Revolutionary War, a committee of the Congress of Confederation, headed by Thomas Jefferson, laid the framework for administering public lands. Ordinances of 1785 and 1787 enabled rapid development of western lands by granting clear ownership to purchasers.

Sale and trade of the public lands furthered Jeffersonian democracy's dream of a nation of independent farmers. The power of government over the land shaped distinctive American attitudes toward government. The founding fathers envisioned a country of citizens free from state and economic tyranny based on each family's possession of a freehold. The dream of being a freeholder is one of the most powerful components of the American character. This dream drove and continues to drive development and resource law. The promise of cheap land easily obtained was central to U.S. political life in the nineteenth century. The idea that an independent freehold is every citizen's dream continues to influence environmental law.

In the 1800s, land was sold on credit; by 1820, the government had $21 million of bad loans. More than ninety cases involving land fraud reached the U.S. Court. Native American Indians were displaced, and slavery continued to influence every factor of western expansion and land development.

In 1849, Congress created a department dedicated to resource development. After the Civil War, "the Great Barbecue" was launched: loggers mowed down the great forest, and the railroads disposed millions of acres of land. As a result of these actions, the American Association for Advancement of Science was formed and the Forest Reserve Act was passed in 1891. And, because of the writings of Thoreau and Emerson, the Sierra Club and the Audubon Society were organized.

The Progressive Era, between 1890 and 1920, saw improved social conditions in an urban industrial society and conservation of western wetlands. However, by the 1890s, urbanization and industrialization transformed U.S. society at the expense of the environment. Thus, the law of nuisance developed, along with smoke ordinances and pollution-abatement regulations.

Then came Theodore Roosevelt, who stated in his autobiography that his conservation program was the most important achievement of his presidency.

World War I put conservation in the background, and there was an emphasis on maximum industrial production. In the 1920s, the courts emphasized zoning laws. One of the most significant achievements of Franklin Delano Roosevelt's New Deal was land and resources restoration. But World War II eclipsed the conservation agenda; production of chemicals rose fivefold, and pollution was dumped on a large scale in the water and on the land.

After World War II, conservation again took a backward step; but between 1948 and 1972, Congress enacted and amended many environmental laws, including amending the Air Pollution Control Act five times.

In the middle 1960s, President Johnson's Congress passed the Wilderness Act in 1964, the Land and Water Conversation Fund Act in 1965, the National Historic Preservation Act in 1966, the Wild and Scenic Rivers Act in 1968, the Endangered Species Act, and the Delaney Act Amendments to the Federal Food and Drug Act.

In the late 1960s, national park visitation reached approximately 200 million visits a year, or the average of one per citizen. From 1969, environmental law grew rapidly, and by Earth Day 1970, environmental issues had become a major political subject. In 1970, Congress passed amendments to the Clean Air Act, created the Occupational Safety and Health Act (OSHA) and the Federal Insecticide Fungicide and Rodenticide Act (FIFRA), among others, and passed the Safe Drinking Water Act in 1974. In addition, the National Environmental Protection Agency Act (NEPA) fostered a synthesis of environmental and economic analysis.

The Energy Crisis of 1973 and the rise in energy prices caused by the Arab oil embargo caused a debate between environmental values and energy concerns. Reagan was not interested in the environment, and there was a gridlock between him and Congress on pollution-control matters. Funding for the Superfund program expired, and many of the EPA's regulations were contested in the courts.

In the 1980s, environmental regulations were reduced, and there was a philosophy of judicial restraint. State environmental law came of age in the 1980s, and many existing environmental programs were implemented and enforced by the use of criminal sanctions.

As a result of changes through the eras, there has been a great deal of change and overly detailed statutes, which have not yet provided adequate protection for the environment.

HINT

You can use *Shepard's Acts and Cases by Popular Name* to quickly find the cite of an act. For example, by using *Shepard's*, you can easily find that the Clean Air Act is located at 42 U.S.C. §74091 ct.seq.

BIBLIOGRAPHY

Loose-Leaf Services

Environment Reporter. Washington, D.C.: Bureau of National Affairs, 1999. This is one of the most comprehensive environmental multivolume loose-leaf services; it has a Current Developments binder that contains weekly reports of national and state news, including legislation, regulations, standards, enforcement, litigation, and proposed regulations. This volume is also on Lexis and Westlaw. There are also volumes entitled *Federal Laws, Federal Regulations*, and *Mining*; a separate Master Index is provided for the *Federal Laws* and for the *Federal Regulations* volumes. Decisions of federal and state courts are published in the *Decisions* volume. Also included is a document delivery service, which is available at 800-452-7773, or 202-452-4323. KF 3775 .A6 .E1 49.

Environmental Law Reporter: A Project of the Environmental Law Institute. Washington, D.C.: The Institute, 1999. This multivolume loose-leaf has a News and Analysis section containing articles, commentaries, new developments, and bibliographies of journal literature; a Pending Litigation section; a section called Statutes; and a section containing Administrative Materials. The Index volume has subject matter indexes, a Table of Cases Index, and a Pending Litigation Index. There is a document delivery service, and consultations with environmental attorneys are also available at 800-443-5120 or 202-939-3844. KF 3775 .A6 .E5.

Frank P. Grad. *Treatise on Environmental Law*. New York: Matthew Bender, 1999. This 5-volume loose-leaf is updated by cumulative supplements. The service covers air pollution, water pollution, solid waste, hazardous waste, Superfund, toxic substances, community right-to-know, noise, radiation, fertilizer and feedlot pollution, pesticides, NEPA, land use, public lands, international aspects, attorneys' fees, and alternative dispute resolution. It also includes a table of cases, and the 2-volume Primary Source Manual includes the text of laws, NEPA regulations, and rules. KF 3775 .G7.

Hornbooks

Celia Campbell-Mohn, ed., Barry Breen, and J. William Futrell. *Environmental Law: From Resources to Recovery*. St. Paul, Minn.: West, 1993, with 1997 pocket part.

William A. Rodgers. *Environmental Law*. 2nd ed. St. Paul, Minn.: West, 1994, with 1998 pocket part. This book offers a detailed and comprehensive treatment of legal principles and issues relating to environmental law, including air pollution, water pollution, FIFRA, toxic substances, hazardous wastes, and Superfund. KF 3775 .R59.

Treatises

Steven Gerrey. *Environmental Law: Examples and Explanations*. New York: Aspen Law and Business, 1997. This treatise considers technical, legal, scientific, and policy aspects of environmental law for practitioners. Topics include administrative procedure, NEPA, constitutional issues, air quality, water pollution, water rights, Resource Conservation and Recovery Act (RCRA), Superfund, local control, wetlands, energy, and the Environmental Site Assessment (ESA). KF 3775 .Z9 .F47.

Nutshells

Roger W. Findley and Daniel A. Farber. *Environmental Law in a Nutshell*. 4th ed. St. Paul, Minn.: West, 1996. This publication covers judicial review, federal and state power, NEPA, pollution control, toxic substances, and preservation of natural areas. KF 3775 .Z9 .F56.

Directories

Environmental Telephone Directory. Rockville, Md.: Government Institutes, 1994. This directory includes the names of U.S. Senators and Representatives, their environmental aides, Senate and House committees, and subcommittees. U.S. Environmental Protection Agency, other federal agencies, and state environmental agencies are included. HC 110 .E5 .E53.

Federal Legislation

Clean Air Act (42 U.S.C. §§ 74091-7671q.) The original Clean Air Act was passed in 1955 (PL 84-159) and was replaced by the Air Quality Act of 1967 (PL 90-148). Amendments were passed in 1970 (PL 91-604), 1977 (PL 95-95), 1983 (PL 98-213), and 1990 (PL 101-549). This act established a system where states prepare and submit plans to implement national clear air standards. If a state implementation plan is approved by the EPA, then the state is primarily responsible for administering the permit program. The EPA is required to comment on environmental impact statements prepared by other agencies.

Clean Water Act (33 U.S.C. §§ 1251-1387). The Clean Water Act of 1977 (PL 92-500) amends the Federal Water Pollution Control Act Amendments of 1972 (PL 92-500, 86 Stat. 816), which basically rewrote federal water pollution law; it was last amended in 1990 (PL 101-596, 101 Stat. 60).

Coastal Zone Management Act (16 U.S.C. §§ 145 1-1464).

Comprehensive Environmental Responses Compensation and Liability Act of 1980 (CERCLA) (PL 96-510, 42 U.S.C §§ 9601-9675, 94 Stat. 2767). This act creates the Superfund. CERCLA was amended in 1986 by the Superfund Amendments and Reauthorization Act of 1986 (SARA) (PL 99-499, 100 Stat. 1613). CERCLA was last amended in 1992 (PL 101-426, 106 Stat. 21745).

Endangered Species Act (16 U.S.C. §§ 1531-1544).

Federal Insecticide, Fungicide, and Rodenticide Act (FIFRA) (7 U.S.C. §§136-136y).

National Environmental Policy Act of 1969 (NEPA). This act was signed on January 1, 1970 (PL 91-190, 42 U.S.C. §§ 4321-4370d, 83 Stat. 852). NEPA requires environmental impact statements from all federal agencies that undertake major federal actions significantly affecting the quality of the human environment. It creates the Council on Environmental Quality (CEQ), which issues regulations that implement the act.

National Forest Management Act (16 U.S.C. §§ 1600-1614).

Resource Conservation and Recovery Act (RCRA) (42 U.S.C. §§6901-6992k).

Safe Drinking Water Act [Public Health Service Act, Title 14] 42 U.S.C. (300f-300j-26).

State Sources

Deborah Hitchcock Jessup. *Guide to State Environmental Programs*. 2nd ed. Washington, D.C.: Bureau of National Affairs, 1994. This guide describes the federal laws and regulations underlying many of the state programs. Then programs for each state (including air pollution, water pollution, and waste management) are described in a state-by-state arrangement. HC 110 .E5 .J47.

Environmental Law Journals

Journal of Energy, Natural Resources, and Environmental Law
Journal of Environmental Law and Litigation
Natural Resources Journal
Ocean Development and International Law Journal

Computer Sources

Westlaw

ENV-TP (full text of law reviews, texts, continuing legal education (CLE) materials, bar journals, and legal practice materials)
ELR-STIA (Environmental Law Reporter–Statutes and International Agreements)
MLRASB (Mealey's Litigation Report–Asbestos)
ELR-LIT (Environmental Law Reporter–Litigation)
FENV-CS (Federal Environmental Law Cases)

Lexis

ENVIRN;ENVLR (full text of law review articles)
ENVIRN;BNAENV (BNA Environmental Reporter Articles)
ENVIRN;CURNWS (current news)
ENVIRN;ELR (Environmental Law Reporter)
ENVIRN;EPAAPP (EPA Appeals Board Decisions)

Internet

The U.S. Environmental Protection Agency World Wide Web Server (http://www.epa.gov) provides the full text of proposed rules and announcements of environmental impact statements from 1999 on. This home page has a database of more than 300 information resources, such as hotlines and clearinghouses. There are also policy and strategy documents and grants.

EcoNet provides access to conferences and news and many environmental topics; it is available at http://www.igc.org/igc/gateway/enindex.html. However, this system is not free.

For court decisions, government documents, and journal articles, see http://www.findlaw.com/01topics/.

For information on the Clean Air Act, see http://www.law.cornell.edu/uscode/42/ch85.html.

ENDNOTES

1. *Environmental Law: From Politics to Recovery* (St. Paul, Minn.: West, 1993).

ASSIGNMENT A

Environmental Law Research

Sources

Shepard's Act and Cases by Popular Names
USCA/USCS and *USCCAN (U.S. Code Congressional and Administrative News)*
Roger Findley, *Environmental Law in a Nutshell*
William Rodgers, *Environmental Law*
Lexis
Westlaw

1. Find the Clean Air Act in the *U.S. Code*. You can look up the act in *Shepard's Act and Cases by Popular Name* to obtain the cite, or you can look up the act in the index to either the *USCA* or the *USCS*. Cite to the original act and to the amendments. When were the amendments passed and what were the public laws for the amendments?

2. What is the "bubble concept" under the Clean Air Act? You can look in *Environmental Law in a Nutshell*, by Roger Findley, or in a hornbook, *Environmental Law,* by William Rodgers, to find a definition.

3. Find the landmark *Chevron* case of 1984. You can use FENVCS on Westlaw or GENFED;OMNI on Lexis. Did the U.S. Supreme Court uphold the use of the bubble? Why? Cite to the case.

4. Look up Public Law 95-95 in *USCCAN*. You can use the Find Key on Westlaw: FI: Type USPL 95-95; or, on Lexis, use LEXSEE 95PL-95 (retrieves only a compressed format, which needs to be extended by downloading on a PDF format). Look up Section 103(d)(1). How much time does each state have to submit a list that identifies air quality control regions?

5. Find a *Law Review* article about *Chevron v. N.R.D.C.* and the "bubble concept." You can look in ENV-TP on Westlaw or ENVIRN;ENVLR on Lexis for an article called Pollution Control by Aiken and Brooks. What was the authors' opinion? Has the U.S. Supreme Court declined to burst the "bubble concept"? What is a "major statutory source"?

ASSIGNMENT B

Environmental Law Research

Sources

BNA Environmental Reporter
Frank L. Grad, *Treatise on Environmental Law*
ELI Environmental Law Reporter

1. Using Frank L. Grad's *Treatise on Environmental Law,* locate NEPA (National Environmental Policy Act). (Hint: Look in Volume 8.) What is the purpose of NEPA? Who shares responsibility for enforcing the act?

2. Using the *BNA Environment Reporter* index, find the National Environmental Policy Act (NEPA) and locate the case that says the U.S. Forest Service must complete an environmental impact statement (EIS) pursuant to NEPA before proceeding with salvage timber sales in a national forest. What is the name of the case?

3. Look in the *Environmental Law Reporter* by ELI, which contains bibliographies of environmental materials. Or search on Lexis (LAWREV;ALLREV) or Westlaw (JLR). Find the 1993 Law Review Bibliography, and locate a law review article by Philip M. Ferester about revitalizing NEPA. Cite the article.

4. Find a format or guidelines for an EIS. There is a piece that discusses guidance and administrative aspects of the EIS filing process. On Lexis, go to the Environmental Library and Environmental Reporter File (ENVIRN;ELR) and search by heading or title: (environmental impact statement) or ti(environmental impact statement). Or you can search on Westlaw by preliminary field or by title in the ELR (Environmental Law Reporter) database: Pr,ti("environmental impact statement"). Cite to the *Environmental Law Reporter*. What is the time period for "review and comment" on environmental impact statements?

5. Search on Westlaw in BNA-ER (Environmental Reporter) for an environmental impact statement form about radioactive waste dated July 17, 1998. How many federal facilities will be chosen for disposing plutonium?

CHAPTER 12

Criminal Law/Criminal Procedure

INTRODUCTION

A crime is any act or omission forbidden by public law in the interest of protecting society that is made punishable by the government in a proceeding brought before it.[1] Punishment for criminal conduct includes fines, imprisonment, probation, and death.[2] In addition, some states have enacted victim indemnification statutes, which establish funds, financed by criminal fines, to provide indemnification in limited amounts to victims of crimes.[3]

Historically, criminal law was primarily case law.[4] Today, however, criminal law is almost exclusively statutory.[5] All states have enacted comprehensive criminal law statutes (or codes) covering most, if not all, of the common law crimes.[6] Because there are not federal common law crimes, all federal crimes are statutory.[7]

In general, a crime consists of two elements: (1) the wrongful or overt act (actus reus), and (2) the criminal or mental intent (mens rea).[8] For example, to support a larceny conviction, one must establish not only that the defendant stole another's goods, but also that the defendant intended to steal the goods.

Conversely, criminal intent without an overt act is not a crime. For instance, Ann decides to rob the neighborhood grocery store and then to really have a great time. With only these facts, Ann has not committed a crime.[9] Just the intention is not enough; there must be an act.

As far as crimes go, in the United States, a burglary is committed every 13 seconds, a rape is committed every 5 minutes, a robbery occurs every 1 minute, and a murder occurs every 30 minutes.[10] These statistics translate into approximately 54 murders a day in the United States (19,500 in 1996); 26 rapes per day (9,490 in 1996); .7 murders per day (256 murders in 1996). In the United States, 1,461 robberies occur per day, or half a million robberies per year; and 6,821 burglaries are committed per day (over 2 million burglaries were committed in 1996).[11]

Before discussing criminal procedure, it is necessary to discuss the difference between criminal law and criminal procedure. The difference is well-illustrated in cases in which a person is found guilty of a particular crime but escapes punishment because the proper procedures weren't used and his or her rights were violated. For example, if the police search a house without a search warrant and they find an illegal drug, the possessor of the drug may go free because there was no warrant. The fact that the possession of the drug is defined as a crime is a substantive criminal law matter, whereas the result of engaging in a warrantless search is a matter of criminal procedure.[12]

Concerning criminal procedure, each of the states and the federal government have procedures for initiating and coordinating criminal prosecutions. In addition, the first ten amendments to the U.S. Constitution, the Bill of Rights, guarantee many defenses and rights of an accused.[13] The Fourth Amendment prohibits unreasonable searches and seizures to obtain incriminating evidence.[14] The Fifth Amendment requires indictment by a grand jury for capital crimes, prevents double jeopardy, protects against self-incrimination, and prohibits deprivation of life or liberty without due process of law.[15] The Sixth Amendment requires that an accused receive a speedy and public trial by an impartial jury, and that the accused be informed of the nature of the accusation, be confronted with the witnesses who testify against him or her, be given the power to obtain witnesses in his or her favor, and have the right to competent counsel for his or her defense.[16] The Eighth Amendment prohibits excessive bail, excessive fines, and cruel or unusual punishment.[17]

Some critical steps in a criminal prosecution are the preliminary hearing, the indictment, the information (criminal complaint), and the arraignment.[18] And finally, the burden in a criminal trial is beyond a reasonable doubt.[19]

HINT

F. Lee Bailey's *Investigation and Preparation of Criminal Cases* is a gold mine of information for a trial lawyer defending a criminal case.

BIBLIOGRAPHY

Loose-Leaf Services

BNA Criminal Law Reporter. Washington, D.C.: Bureau of National Affairs, 1999. This multi-volume loose-leaf has a topical index, a table of cases, and summaries of significant court opinions. The *Reporter* is updated weekly and has comprehensive and extremely current news in the criminal law area. KF 9615 .C7.

Criminal Law Bulletin. Boston, Mass.: Warren, Gorham, and LaMont, 1978–1999. This bulletin has articles and features from top authorities on criminal law. It contains the latest federal and state decisions in every phase of criminal law. K3 .R5.

Treatises

F. Lee Bailey. *Complete Manual of Criminal Forms: Federal and State*. Rochester, N.Y.: Lawyers' Cooperative Publishing, 1963. This manual contains over 1,000 federal and state criminal forms. There are pretrial and posttrial proceedings. Contents include arrest and arraignment, motions, stipulations, affidavits, orders, elements of the crime, evidentiary matters, and so on. KF 9616 .B25.

F. Lee Bailey. *Cross-Examination in Criminal Trials*. Rochester, N.Y.: Lawyers' Cooperative Publishing, 1978. This book discusses in detail the Sixth Amendment Confrontation Clause with the inclusion of a right of cross-examination. Bailey's *Cross-Examination* also delves into the Fourteenth Amendment. This treatise has examples of actual cross-examination with trial techniques. KF 9658 .B28.

F. Lee Bailey. *Investigation and Preparation of Criminal Cases*. Rochester, N.Y.: Lawyers' Cooperative Publishing, 1985. This is the most complete and up-to-date guide to investigations for the trial lawyer defending a criminal case. KF 9655 .B3.

Francis Wharton. *Wharton's Criminal Law*. Rochester, N.Y.: Lawyers' Cooperative Publishing, 1978. This 4-volume treatise thoroughly examines and analyzes every phase of criminal law—in both state and federal jurisdictions. *Wharton's* clarifies the principles underlying today's criminal law practice and has an in-depth discussion of the Model Penal Code. KF 9219 .W43.

Francis Wharton. *Wharton's Criminal Procedure*. Rochester, N.Y.: Lawyers' Cooperative Publishing, 1978. This is the twin treatise to *Wharton's Criminal Law* and analyzes criminal procedure through the federal constitution, the Fourteenth Amendment, and the Bill of Rights. KF 9619 .W43.

Digests

Criminal Law Digest. St. Paul, Minn.: West, 1985. This digest contains significant cases from all fifty states and all federal jurisdictions. KF9210.3 .C75 1983.

James A. Douglas. *Criminal Law Digest: State, Federal, Constitutional Law and Procedure: A Topically Classified Digest of Significant Decisions on Criminal Law and Procedure*. Boston, Mass.: Warren, Gorham, and LaMont, 1983. This is a one-volume digest of cases with thorough explanations, a table of cases, and a topical index. KF 9210.3 .C75.

Codes

Federal Criminal Code. St. Paul, Minn.: West, 1998. This contains the federal rules, motion attaching sentence rules, evidence, appellate procedure, and Supreme Court rules. KF 9606.99 .D567.

Hornbooks

Wayne LaFave and Austin Scott, Jr. *Criminal Law*. 2nd ed. St. Paul, Minn.: West, 1986, with 1998 pocket part. This hornbook examines the basic sources, appellate opinions, and statutes with critical commentary. There is an emphasis on techniques of legal analysis. Attention is also given to the Model Penal Code. KF 9219 .L38.

Rollin M. Perkins. *Criminal Law*. 3rd ed. New York: Foundation Press, 1982. This is a basic hornbook with multiple references to the Model Penal Code. KF9219 .P4 1982.

Richard G. Singer. *Criminal Law: Examples and Explanations*. New York: Aspen Publishing, 1997. This publication is designed to provide accurate and authoritative examples and information on such crimes as rape, theft, conspiracy, and so on. KF 9219.3 .S54.

Wayne R. LaFave and Jerold H. Israel. *Criminal Procedure*. 2nd ed. St. Paul, Minn.: West, 1992, with 1998 pocket part. This hornbook covers the laws governing all the major steps in the criminal justice process, starting with investigation and ending with postappeal collateral attacks. KF9219 .L38 1986.

Robert M. Bloom and Mark S. Brodin. *Criminal Procedure: Examples and Explanations*. 2nd ed. Boston, Mass.: Aspen Publishing, 1996. This book begins with a short overview of criminal procedure followed by chapters on the Fourth, Fifth, and Sixth Amendments. It also includes expanded introductory material on state constitutional protection, a new section on entrapment, and new problems and material to reflect all the latest developments. KF9630 .Z9 .B58 1996.

Nutshells

Jerold H. Israel and Wayne R. LaFave. *Criminal Procedure—Constitutional Limitations in a Nutshell*. 5th ed. St. Paul, Minn.: West, 1993. This nutshell provides a succinct analysis of the constitutional standards of major current significance. KF9619.3 .I8 1993.

Arnold H. Loewy. *Criminal Law in a Nutshell*. 2nd ed. St. Paul, Minn.: West, 1987. This book gives a succinct explanation of substantive criminal law with case citations and explanations. KF 9219.3 .L63.

State Criminal Materials

(will vary by state)

Computer Sources

Westlaw

FCJ-CS (Federal Criminal Justice Cases)
ULA-MPC (Uniform Laws Annotated-Model Penal Code)

Lexis

CRIME;MEGA (Combined Federal and State Cases)
CRIME;USRULE (Federal Rules Annotated)

Internet

Criminal justice: Vera Institute of Justice: http://www.vera.org
Criminal law and related resources: http://www.law.cornell.edu/topics/criminal.html
Penal law: http://wings.buffalo.edu/law/bclc/web/cover

ENDNOTES

1. Richard A. Mann and Barry S. Roberts, *Essentials of Business Law and the Legal Environment* (St. Paul, Minn.: West, 1995), 94.
2. Ibid., 94-95.
3. Ibid., 95.
4. Ibid.
5. Ibid.
6. Ibid.
7. Ibid.
8. Ibid.
9. Ibid.
10. FBI statistics as quoted in the *Birmingham Post*, November 23, 1998.
11. *Statistical Abstract of the United States* (Washington, D.C.: Department of Commerce, Bureau of the Census), 212.
12. Stephen Elias and Susan Levinkind, *Legal Research: How to Find and Understand the Law* (Berkeley: Nolo Press, 1997), 4/5.
13. Mann and Roberts, 104.
14. Ibid.
15. Ibid.
16. Ibid.
17. Ibid.
18. Ibid.
19. Ibid.

ASSIGNMENT A

Criminal Law/Criminal Procedure

Sources

Bailey, *Investigation and Preparation of Criminal Cases*
BNA Criminal Law Reporter
Wharton's Criminal Law
Wharton's Criminal Evidence
Federal Criminal Code
West's *Federal Practice Digest*, 3rd ed.
Lexis
Westlaw

Kenny and Ann were driving down the highway on the way to his sister's birthday party when they stopped at a roadblock. Kenny has mild cerebral palsy, which causes his speech to be slurred and also affects his balance and coordination. When the police officer at the roadblock saw Kenny, he thought Kenny was drunk or on drugs and asked Kenny to step out of the car. Then the officer began to search Kenny and Kenny's car for drugs and found an envelope of marijuana in Kenny's pocket and some marijuana and experimental drugs on the floor of the car behind the driver's seat. There was a question of whether the marijuana was obtained for medical purposes. Kenny was charged.

1. With what crimes would Kenny be charged? (Hint: Try the Federal Criminal Code.)

2. Is Kenny intoxicated? Look in *Wharton's Criminal Law* and find a definition of intoxication. What does *Wharton's* say is the appropriate Model Penal Code Section?

3. Find the *BNA Criminal Law Reporter* index, 4/1/98–3/31/99. Locate and name a district case from Utah that discusses "mistaking a mild neurological disorder for intoxication." What happened to the suit? What type of person was involved? Under what act was the suit brought? Where in the *BNA Criminal Law Reporter* did you find the entry?

4. Look in *Wharton's Criminal Evidence*, page 614. Is it relevant to show the conduct of the defendant subsequent to the crime, in the instant case, open possession of marijuana, even if such conduct indicates a consciousness of guilt? Cite to a 5th Circuit case.

5. Can Ann testify as to whether Kenny was under the influence? Using F. Lee Bailey's *Investigation and Preparation of Criminal Cases*, find out whether a nonexpert witness may testify if a defendant was or was not under the influence of alcohol at the time of the accident in question. What is the section in Bailey?

6. Were Kenny's Fourth Amendment rights violated? Use Westlaw (ALLFEDS), Lexis (GENFED;MEGA) or West's *Federal Law Practice*, 3rd ed., to locate *Terry v. Ohio*. Cite the case and explain the holding, including the two-part test.

ASSIGNMENT B

Criminal Procedure

Use the same fact pattern as in Assignment A, except do the search in your state jurisdiction.

Sources for Virginia (for example; sources will vary)

Code of Virginia
Drug Cases in Virginia
Criminal Cases in Virginia
Criminal Offenses and Defenses in Virginia
Virginia Criminal Procedure
Model Jury Instructions
West's Virginia Digest
Wharton's Criminal Evidence

1. With what crimes will the defendant be charged?

2. Find a definition of possession. (Hint: Try *Defending Drug Cases* or *Model Jury Instructions*.)

3. Is Kenny intoxicated? (Hint: Find the appropriate state code section.)

4. Is it relevant to show the conduct of the defendant subsequent to the crime, even if such conduct indicates a consciousness of guilt? Use *Wharton's Criminal Evidence* and cite to the *Harrell* case.

5. Is there a case in your state that discusses mistaking a mild neurological disorder for intoxication? (Hint: Try a digest, *BNA's Criminal Law Reporter,* or Westlaw, ALLFEDS, or Lexis, GENFED;COURTS.)

6. Can Ann testify as to whether Kenny was under the influence? (Hint: Try F. Lee Bailey's *Investigation and Preparation of Criminal Cases.*)

7. Were Kenny's Fourth Amendment rights violated? Was there probable cause? (Hint: Try *Defending Criminal Cases in Virginia.*)

CHAPTER 13

Westlaw

INTRODUCTION

In 1870, John B. West, age 20, began selling office supplies, dictionaries, legal forms, and law treatises.[1] Because St. Paul lawyers who bought West's wares complained that it took too long to obtain published court proceedings, John, and his brother, Horatio, launched a weekly newspaper that contained court opinions. By 1879, the West brothers were publishing court opinions from Iowa, Michigan, Nebraska, Wisconsin, and the Dakota Territory.[2] By the turn of the century, the company formed by the West brothers was publishing regional reports nationwide, as well Supreme Court decisions.[3]

In 1973, the management of the West Publishing Company decided to enter the market with a computer system of its own—Westlaw.[4] The first Westlaw subscriber went online in April 1975.[5]

The initial Westlaw system was very primitive; the software was balky and unreliable, and the database consisted solely of West headnotes. In 1976, West began building a full-text database that would consist of both the full text of judicial opinions and the West headnotes.[6] However, searches were slow and were frequently interrupted by hardware problems or difficulties with communications networks. By 1980, West began a thorough redesign of Westlaw, including search time in a few seconds.[7] By 1984, virtually all of the software problems had been solved, and Westlaw was a highly sophisticated, user-friendly research service.[8]

HINTS

1. Use the books first to get an idea of search terms—you will save time.
2. Formulate your query on paper before you sign on—you can save as much as $20.00 by doing this.

WESTLAW LOGIC

Formulate your query (search) before you sign on and use key words.

Root Expanders ! and *

! is used to indicate variation of words. For example, deduct! will generate deducted, deducting, deduction, and so on.

* is used to generate a certain number of letters or for irregular words. For example, m*n generates man or men.

Boolean Operators

"or" is a space.
"and" is an ampersand (&).
"/n" refers to a number of words you choose between terms.

For example, set-off deduct! /15 back-pay, will result in fifteen words between deduct and back-pay.

Grammatical Operators

/p
/s

Phrase Searching

"statute of liberty"
"statute of limitations"

Putting the Query Together

discrim! & set-off deduct! /p back-pay /p unemployment

db (database)	sdb (switch database)
gb (go back)	kw (kwic cite)
map	1(locate)

Field Searching

title	ti(Nock)
attorney	at(Denison)
judge	ju(ginsburg)
court	co(fl)
synopsis	sy,di(drug /s inform! /p immun!)

Digest

citation	ci(100 +5 1189)	Fi 118 U.S. 904 (Find)

Date Restriction

da(1992)	da(<1985)
da(aft 1990 & bef 1993)	da(before 1992)
da(aft aug. 1, 1990)	da(bef 10-1-86)

Databases

Allfeds
Allstates
  Pa-cs
Key Cite or KC (for *Shepard's*)
JLR (Journals and law reviews)
WIN (Westlaw is Natural)
1-800-Westlaw or 1-800-688-6363 (reference attorneys)

Internet

www.westlaw.com

ENDNOTES

1. Sharon Schmickle, "West Has a Long Publishing History," *Star Tribune (Minneapolis)*, 1.
2. Ibid.
3. Ibid.
4. *Computer-Assisted Legal Research*, 77 Law Library Journal 553 (1984-85).
5. Ibid.
6. Ibid., 554.
7. Ibid.
8. Ibid.

ASSIGNMENT A

Advanced Westlaw Research

In recent decades, the Florida citrus industry has used Red No. 2 and Red No. 32 to color oranges without harmful effects on humans. This use of coloring agents has been pursuant to the Federal Food and Drug Administration's regulations as authorized by the Federal Food, Drug, and Cosmetic Act.

After eating a Florida orange, our client, Mrs. Brashford, developed a severe rash over her entire body and suffered a cardiac arrest. She became so ill that she required hospitalization for two days. Mrs. Brashford wants to know whether she can sue the Florida Citrus Commission for false advertising, breach of warranty, negligence, or any other cause of action for saying "how healthy it is to eat Florida oranges." She wants to file a claim in Federal Circuit Court, because her hospital bill was $77,000. Develop a search strategy (query), finding out whether the citrus industry has complied with the law concerning coloring and labeling, and report to the senior partner whether we should take the case.

Some applicable databases on Westlaw are:

ALLFEDS/CTA (Federal cases/Circuit Court)
CFR/FR (Code of Federal Register/Federal Register)
LH (Federal Legislative History)
JLR (Journals and Law Reviews)
USCA (United States Code Annotated)
ALR (American Law Reports)

ASSIGNMENT B

Advanced Westlaw Research

Same assignment as Lexis Assignment B, but use Westlaw.
Some appropriate databases are

ALLFEDS
JLR (Journals and Law Reviews)
TP-ALL (Texts and Periodicals)
LH (Legislative History)
USCA (United States Code Annotated)
ALR
CFR/FR (Code of Federal Regulation/Federal Register)
FTX-ALL (Federal Tax Cases, Regulations, Statutes, Letter Rulings)
FTX-CS (Federal Tax Cases)

CHAPTER 14

Lexis

INTRODUCTION

Lexis began in the late 1960s as a project of the Ohio State Bar Association, which wanted to put the case law of Ohio and other states onto a centralized computer, so that remote users could search case law by any word or phrase.[1] The Ohio State Bar Association contracted with Data Corporation, a small Ohio high-tech company, to build a system to do this. In 1968, before the project got under way, Data Corporation was acquired by the Mead Corporation, a large paper and printing manufacturer located in Dayton, Ohio. Mead formed a division, Mead Data Central, to develop the service, and under this name, launched the service nationally in 1973. Initially, the system contained the case law of three states (New York, Ohio, and Missouri), federal case law, and federal statutes.

Mead Data Central has added materials to Lexis year by year, until the system of libraries and files contains today almost all useful case law, statutes, and news (Nexis).

Lexis/Nexis services contain more than 343 gigabytes of information. (A gigabyte is one thousand megabytes of one billion characters of information.) So, Lexis/Nexis contains 343 billion characters worth of searchable information, or over 170 million pages of information. There are nearly 3,900 different files, and more than 650,000 documents are added each week to the 188 million documents online. There are 370,000 active subscribers. In 1992, Lexis/Nexis had annual sales of about $495 million.

You can search Lexis on the Internet at http://www.lexis.com.

HINTS

1. Don't forget that Lexis has a two-point entry: Libraries and Files.
2. Statistics have shown that searches done with Boolean logic produce better and more accurate results than Freestyle.
3. Formulate your search before going online. You can save as much as $20.00 by doing this.
4. Go to the books first and find key terms. Your research will be more thorough. Book research has still been shown to produce better results than computer research.

LEXIS LOGIC

Root Expanders ! and *

! is used to indicate variation of words. For example, constitution! will generate constitutional, constitutionality, and so on.

* is used to generate a limited number of characters or for irregular words. For example, wom*n* and m*n will generate woman or women and man or men.

Boolean Operators

Or on Lexis is "or"; it is used for synonyms. For example, drunk or intoxicated will retrieve any document containing either one of these terms.

And on Lexis is "and". For example, "roadblock and constitutional" will retrieve any document that has both the terms *roadblock* and *constitutional* in it.

"w/n" refers to a certain number you choose. For example, roadblock w/15 constitutional will retrieve only those documents where *roadblock* is within 15 words of the term *constitutional.*

Phrase Searching

statute of limitations
dead storage

There are grammatical connectors as w/s (within the same sentence) or w/p (within the same paragraph), as on Westlaw.

Sample Search

roadblock or checkpoint w/20 drunk or intox! or sobriety w/20 constitution! or unconstitution! and advance or prior w/5 notice or publicity

Some Commands

Searching

cl	change library
.cf	change file
.ns	new search
.m	modify search
.so	sign off
.es	leave Shepard's

Viewing

.fu	full format
.kw	kwic format
.ci	cite format

Reviewing Document

.np	next page
.pp	previous page
.fp	first page
.nd	next document
.fd	display document

Printing

.pr	print document
.pa	print all

Signing Off

.so

Date Restrictions

date is 5/22/78	=
date aft 1977	>
date bef 1980	<

Segment Searching

Name(finberg)
Writtenby(ginsburg) opinionby(marshall)
Number(76-1800)
Counsel(denison)
Cite(436 pre/5 268)

Libraries/Files

Genfed;Omni
States;Omni
Lawrev;Allrev

Citators

Shep (Shepard's)
ic (Instacite)
.sp (Shepard's Preview)
Freestyle (non-Boolean searching)

Internet

www.lexis.com

Lexis Customer Service

1-800-543-6862

ENDNOTES

1. Stephen Emmanuel, *Lexis for Law Students* (Larchmont, N.Y.: Emmanuel Law Outlines, 1994.

ASSIGNMENT A

Advanced Lexis Research

Use the same information as in Assignment A in the Advanced Westlaw Research. Develop a search strategy and report to the senior partner whether we should take the case.

Some applicable libraries and files are

GENFED;USAPP OR COURTS
CODES;CFR
LEGIS;BLTRCK
LAWREV;ALLREV
GENFED;USCS
NEWS;CURNWS
ALR;ALR

Some possible searches are

red w/ 10 color or dye w/20 food
red and dye w/20 color w/3 red
red pre/5 color or dye w/10 food

ASSIGNMENT B

Advanced Lexis Research

Rawley and DeFalice Law Firm has selected you to research the Technical and Miscellaneous Revenue Act of 1988 (TAMRA), which was created by the IRS. This act deals with tax laws regarding allowance for obsolescence in trade or business. Our client owned two very expensive, rare books with rare lithographic prints. One of the books was damaged when a severe storm caused damage to his house. The client wants to know if he can claim a tax deduction under TAMRA. The senior partner needs case law, law reviews, the statute, and any relevant information that you can find on the act. Thoroughly explain your search strategy and research, and report to the partner whether our client can claim the depreciation deduction.

Some appropriate libraries and files are:

GENFED;USCS OR GENFED;COURTS
LAWREV;ALLREV
ALR;ALR
CODES;CFR
NEWS;CURNWS
GENFED;TC (Tax Court)
GENFED;CASES

A COMPARISON OF LEXIS AND WESTLAW

Lexis	Westlaw
Root expanders ! *	Root expanders ! *
Boolean operators "or" is or	Boolean operators "or" is a space
"and" is and	"and" is &
"w/n" refers to a number of words you choose between the next term	"/n" refers to a number of words you choose between the next term

Phrase Searching

Lexis	Westlaw
dead storage	dead storage

Grammatical Connectors

Lexis	Westlaw
w/s (within the same sentence)	/s (within the same sentence)
w/p (within the same paragraph)	/p (within same paragraph)

Field Searching

Lexis	Westlaw
name (Finberg)	ti(Finberg)
written by (Ginsburg)	ju(Ginsburg)
opinion by (Ginsburg)	
counsel (Denison)	at(Denison)
court (Florida)	co(Fl)
Ci (436 pre/5 268)(436 comes before 268)	Ci (436 + 5 268)(436 comes before 268)

Date Restriction

Lexis	Westlaw
Date is 05/22/78	Da (05/22/78)
Date aft 1977	Da (aft 1977)
Date bef 1980	Da bef (1980)

Dot Commands

Lexis	Westlaw
.so (sign off)	off (sign off)
.pa (print all)	pr (print)
.pr (print document)	

CHAPTER 15

Internet

INTRODUCTION

The Internet was started in 1969 under a contract let by the Advanced Research Projects Agency (ARPA), which connected four major computers at universities in the southwestern United States: University of California at Los Angeles, Stanford Research Institute, University of Southern California at Berkeley, and the University of Utah.[1] University of Cambridge, Massachusetts, carried out the contract.[2] By 1970, Massachusetts Institute of Technology (MIT) and Harvard were added; and by 1971, Stanford University, CarnegieMellon, and Case Western Reserve University joined, along with NASA.[3] The Internet was designed in part to provide a communications network that would work even if some of the sites were destroyed by nuclear attack.[4] Early on, the Internet was used by computer experts, engineers, and scientists. There was nothing friendly about it.

For the first decade that the Internet was in existence, it was primarily used to facilitate e-mail, support online discussion groups, allow access to distant databases, and support the transfer of files among government agencies, companies, and universities.[5]

During the early 1980s, all the interconnected research networks were converted to the TCP/IP protocol (which enabled all of the networks to send data back and forth).[6] The ARPANET, as the Internet was originally called, became the backbone (the physical connection between the major sites) of the new Internet, which comprised all TCP/IP based networks.[7] The conversion to TCP/IP was completed by the end of 1983, and the Internet was born.[8]

In 1990, HTML, a hypertext Internet protocol, which could communicate the graphic information on the Internet, was introduced.[9] Each individual could create graphic pages (a Web site), which then became part of a huge, virtual hypertext network called the World Wide Web (WWW).[10] The enhanced Internet was informally renamed the Web, and a huge additional audience was created.[11]

At the moment, most people use the term *Internet* to refer to the physical structure of the Net, including client and server computers and the phone lines that connect everything.[12]

Since the Internet was initially funded by the government, it was originally limited to research, education, and government uses.[13] Commercial uses were prohibited unless they directly served the goals of research and education. This policy continued until the early 1990s, when independent commercial networks began to grow.[14] AOL, Prodigy, and CompuServe came online. It then became possible to route traffic across the country from one commercial site to another without passing through the government-funded Internet backbone. Today, public schools from K though 12 and public libraries have access in addition to the massive, high-volume commercial connections. Free services, supported by advertising, have shifted some of the direct costs away from the consumer, and there are free Web pages, chat rooms, and message boards.

HINTS

1. Web addresses ending in ".com" are commercial, and Web addresses ending in ".edu" are educational.
2. The local public library has free Internet connections.

BIBLIOGRAPHY

Business

Moody's on the Internet is
http://www.moodys.com
CNN on the Internet is
http://www.cnn.com

Bankruptcy

Chapter 7 Bankruptcy is a comprehensive listing of bankruptcy-related resources, including cases, statutes, and other information:
http://www.chapter7.com

Tax

SBTtek Law and Tax Website Directory, or the Digital Daily—IRS is the Internal Revenue Service's home page on the World Wide Web. The goal this Website is to provide immediate access to IRS tax information and services.
http://www.sbt.net/law.html

Patents and Trademarks

IBM Intellectual Property Network:
http://www.patents.ibm.com
U.S. Patent and Trademark Office:
http://www.uspto.gov
For trademarks, search
http://www.ggmark.com
For Intellectual Property Magazine, search
http://www.ipmag.com

Employment/Labor Law

For Employment Discrimination, search the Cornell Law School home page:
http://www.law.cornell.edu

Securities Law

Eaton Vance Online contains mutual funds, taxes, investing, financial, municipals, high yield, tax efficient, tax managed, planning, advice, bank loans, retirement, and assets:
http://www.eatonvance.com

International Law

U.S. Department of State:
http://www.his.com/pildb
http://www.state.gov/www/regions/background_info_countries.html

Medical

Medline contains over 8,000,000 records from over 7,300 different medical and health-related publications:
http://medline.cos.com

Wills and Estates

The National Association of Estate Planning Attorneys Website offers question-and-answer databases on numerous estate planning topics:
http://www.netplanning.com

Government Documents/Legislative Histories

Thomas is the U.S. Congress on the Internet; this home page has current U.S. federal legislative information, including bills, laws, the Congressional Record, reports, and links to further information:
http://thomas.loc.gov
Legislative histories can be found through the Superintendent of Documents home page at
http://www.access.gpo.gov/su_docs

Environmental

U.S. Environmental Protection Agency World Wide Web Server provides the full text of rules, regulations, legislation, proposed rules, and announcements of environmental impact statements from 1999 on. This list serve has a database of more than 300 information resources, such as databases, hotlines, and clearinghouses. There are also policy and strategy documents and grants.
http://www.epa.gov

Criminal

Criminal Law is available through Cornell University:
http://www.law.cornell.edu/topics/criminal.html
Penal law is available at
http://wings.buffalo.edu/law/bclc/web/cover
Westlaw:
http://www.westlaw.com
Lexis:
http://www.lexis.com

Other

Library of Congress:
  http://www.loc.gov./homepage/1chp.html
U.S. Federal Courts:
  http://www.uscourts.gov
ABA:
  http://www.abanet.org
Law Journals Network:
  http://www.lawnewsnetwork.com
Florida Supreme Court:
  http://www.alllaw.com/state_resources/florida/courts

ENDNOTES

1. Walt Howe, *A Brief History of the Internet*, 1999. (Available at http://www.delphi.com.)
2. Ibid.
3. Ibid.
4. Ibid.
5. Kyla Wendell, *The Student Connection Program*, University of Regina, 1997, 1.
6. Ibid.
7. Ibid.
8. Ibid.
9. Ibid.
10. Ibid.
11. Ibid.
12. Ibid.
13. Howe, 3.
14. Ibid.
15. Ibid.

ASSIGNMENT A

Internet Research

Sources

Thomas: http://thomas.loc.gov
Florida Supreme Court: http://www.alllaw.com/state_resources
Library of Congress: http://www.loc.gov

1. Go to Thomas, which is the U.S. Congress on the Internet. This list serve has federal legislative information, including bills, laws, the Congressional Record, reports, and links to further information. Now go to the 106th Congress, and find a house bill that was sponsored by Representative Conyers to prevent violence against women.

   a. What is the bill number?

   b. When was the bill introduced?

   c. What is the short title of the bill?

2. Surf the Internet and find the Library of Congress home page. Go into the Library of Congress Card Catalog Browse Search, and find *Intellectual Property Law* by Dratler. Search by the book title.

   a. What is the call number (KF number)?

   b. What is the date of publication?

   c. What is the place of publication and publisher?

3. Find the Florida Supreme Court list serve, which has links to the Florida Court System. Locate the *Abella v. Rubino* case.

   a. What is the date of the decision?

   b. What is the Circuit?

   c. Did the Eleventh Circuit affirm or reverse the decision of the district court?

ASSIGNMENT B

Internet Research

Sources

U.S. Federal Courts home page: http://www.uscourts.gov
ABA home page: http://www.abanet.org
Law Journals Network: http://www.lawnewsnetwork.com

1. Go to the U.S. Federal Courts home page. Go into "About the U.S. Courts," "Understanding the Federal Courts," and "Courts of Appeals." Find the directory.

   a. What circuit is Pennsylvania?

   b. What is the location of the Third Circuit?

2. Go to the ABA home page. Find the Lawyer Locator. Search for Donald Gerbach.

   a. Where does he practice?

   b. When was he admitted to the Pennsylvania bar?

   c. Where did he go to law school?

3. Go to the Law Journals Network Website. Find the story about divorce lawyer, Jack Jacobson.

   a. What happened to him?

   b. What percentage of family law lawyers have been threatened?

Answer Key

CHAPTER 1

Business Resources

Assignment A

ANSWER 1:
Using the example of Exxon Corporation with the *Million Dollar Directory*, you will find the address and telephone are 225 Lyndon B. Johnson Freeway, Irving, Texas 75063-3705, 214/444-1000. Exxon was founded in 1882; its bank is the Bank of America; the CEO and president is Lee Raymond; the state of incorporation is New Jersey; sales are $118,000,000,000, and there are 79,000 employees.

Using *Standard and Poor's Register of Corporations, Directors and Executives*, you will find about the same information as the *Million Dollar Directory*, except that *Standard and Poor's* lists the 1999 revenues/assets as $118 billion; they list 79,000 employees, 14 vice presidents, 3 senior vice presidents, and counsel as C. W. Matthews.

You can look up on the company's annual report to find similar information. Online, you can use *SEC Edgar*, which is available through Internet and is free at your local public library. There are 88 drilling wells in the United States.

Use Lexis or Westlaw to determine whether the company has been involved in other litigation. Search:

ti(Heinz) on Westlaw in Allfeds or Allstates or
name(Heinz) on Lexis in Genfed or States

Yes, the company has been involved in other litigation.
Value Line will tell you that the total revenues are $92,630,000,000 and the share earnings are $0.41 per share.

Using *SEC Edgar*, you can find that there are 88 drilling wells.

To find a relevant new article about the company, use Lexis (NEWS;ALLNEWS), Westlaw (JLR), or the following database that is available free at your local public library: Infotrac. You can also use Internet search engines such as http://www.altavista.com or http://www.yahoo.com.

Note: Exxon Corporation has its own Web page on the Internet. Most of this information is available on Exxon's Web page, located at http://www.exxon.com.

Assignment B

ANSWER 1:
Grated horseradish was Heinz's first product, which was packed in clear, rather than colored, glass to show its purity.

ANSWER 2:
Weight Watchers is the largest weight loss program and has 4,000,000 members.

ANSWER 3:
Star-Kist Foods, Inc.

ANSWER 4:
Ken-L-Ration and Kibbles and Bits

ANSWER 5:
Orlando Tomate Frito Sauce

ANSWER 6:
Olivine in Zimbabwe produces oil and soap.

ANSWER 7:
50%

ANSWER 8:
759 9/16 (This figure could vary.)

ANSWER 9:
down 5/16 (This figure could vary.)

ANSWER 10:
A decrease

ANSWER 11:
The president and CEO is William R. Johnson.

ANSWER 12:
Baby food

ANSWER 13:
$1.7 billion

CHAPTER 2

Bankruptcy Law

Assignment A

ANSWER 1:
Smiley v. First National Bank of Belleville, 864 F.2d 562 (7th Cir. 1989) as cited in 6 *Collier on Bankruptcy* ¶727.02(6)(a) (15th ed.) 1999.

ANSWER 2:
Toderelli v. Visigraph Typewriter Mfg. Co., 34 F.Supp. 762 (S.D.N.Y. 1940) as cited in 2 *CCH Bankruptcy L. Rep.* §9529A.25 (1995).

ANSWER 3:
1 *Herzog's Bankruptcy Forms and Practice*, pp. 3-24, (1994).

ANSWER 4:
Cheri L. Cohen, *Is the Constitutional Wall for Bankruptcy Court Jurisdiction Crumbling?: Celotex Corp. v. Edwards*, 7 *Norton Bankr. Law Advisor* 4 June 1995.

Assignment B

ANSWER 1:
Bankruptcy Code, section 522(d)(4) (Collier Pamphlet Edition), states that the following property may be exempt under section 522(b)(1):

> The debtor's aggregate interest, not to exceed $1,000 in value, in jewelry held primarily for the personal, family, or household use of the debtor, or a dependent of the debtor.

If the value of the necklace is $6,000, the claim is fully secured with a surplus of $1,000 that constitutes the debtor's equity in the property. The equity is exemptable by Opal under section 522(d)(4), which provides for a $1,000 exemption in jewelry held personal, family, or household use. If Olga has claimed the ring as exempt, she may redeem the ring by paying Unlimited the amount of its secured claim of $5,000 in cash.

Section 722 of the *Bankruptcy Code* (Collier Pamphlet Edition) states that an individual debtor may, whether or not the debtor has waived the right to redeem under this section, redeem tangible personal property from a lien securing a dischargeable consumer debt, if such property is exempted under section 522 of this title, or has been abandoned under section 554 of this title, by paying the holder of such lien the amount of the allowed secured claim of such holder that is secured by such lien.

Here, Opal is an individual; the necklace is tangible personal property; the necklace is for personal use; the debt is a consumer debt, secured in order to discharge consumer debt; the debt is dischargeable; and the property is exempt.

A debtor may redeem collateral securing a debt by paying the creditor the amount of the secured claim or the fair market value of the collateral. *In the Matter of Edwards*, 901 F.2d 1383 (7th Cir. 1990) or 23 C.B.C.2d 488 (Bankr. 7th Cir. 1990).

Assignment C

ANSWER 1:
11 Norton Bankruptcy Law and Practice, §5 Order for Relief Under Chapter 11, p. 19.

ANSWER 2:
David G. Epstein, *Bankruptcy*, St. Paul, Minnesota, West Publishing Co., 1993. Page 616 explains that §522(d)(5) is known as the "Wild Card" exemption, which allows the debtor to exempt her aggregate interest in any property, not to exceed in value $400, plus up to $3,750 of any unused portion of the §522(d)(1) exemption covering property used as a residence.

ANSWER 3:
Use Volume 24 of *West's Bankruptcy Digest* to find the headnote and key number—Bankr. 2895. Go to the squib–S.D.N.Y. 1989; the cite is *In Re Chateaugay Corp.*, 104 B.R. 617 (1989). The LTV Corporation and 66 of its subsidiaries filed for bankruptcy. The complaint alleged a claim of title to certain real property owned by LTV and sought (1) a determination to quiet title; (2) an accounting with respect to all coal mined from the property, and (3) damages in an amount equal to the value of the coal mined by the debtors.

ANSWER 4:
6 Collier Bankruptcy Practice Guide ¶93.50(9)(a), pp. 93-67, 1998.

CHAPTER 3

Tax Law

Assignment A

ANSWER 1:
Using the *CCH Standard Federal Tax Reporter*, Volume 10, 1998, you will find a subject for "like-kind property defined" under ¶31,508.02 -31, 508.0126. There is also a subject heading under "real property" ¶31,508.0127 that says like-kind refers to the nature or character of the property and not to its grade or quality. ¶31,508.0128 says the fact that two properties are both real property is not enough to make them like-kind property. The rights on the properties, and not just the properties themselves, must be similar. Exchange of property held for productive use or investment cite to the Stand. Fed. Rep. (CCH) ¶31,508.012-31,508.0126.

Using the volume 1, Index, *U.S. Tax Reporter* by RIA, you will find a reference to like-kind exchanges in Internal Revenue Code §1031(a)—nonrecognition of gain or loss from exchanges solely in kind.

ANSWER 2:
See *Revenue Ruling* 97-21 (p. 121, IRS Cumulative Bulletin, 1997-1, January-June):

Issue—Whether a hospital violates the requirements for exemption from Federal Income Tax when it provides incentives to recruit private practice physicians to join its medical staff or to provide medical services in the community.

Holding—The hospitals have not violated the requirements for exemption from Federal Income Tax.

Assignment B

ANSWER 1:
Leon H. Perlin Co., Inc., v. Commissioner, 65 T.C.M. (CCH) 2013 (1993).

ANSWER 2:
Critchfield v. Central National Bank of Cleveland, 32 T.C. 844 (1959) I.R.C. §2056.

ANSWER 3:
Lexis: FEDTAX;LEGIS: federal w/3 excise w/3 tax and date is June 1994.
Westlaw: BNA-TRACK C federal /3 excise /3 tax & da(June 1994).
Cigarettes, alcohol, and highways are subject to excise taxes.

ANSWER 4:
Taxpayers were not entitled to depreciation because they did not establish a basis in program copyright and the copyright became worthless.

CHAPTER 4

Patent, Trademark, and Copyright Law

Assignment A

ANSWER 1:
Yes, (Volume) 5 *Nimmer on Copyright*, §21.01(I).

ANSWER 2:
No, (Volume) 5 §21.01 (I), *Nimmer on Copyright*.

ANSWER 3:
No, (Volume) 1 *Nimmer on Copyright*, §1.02 (4).

ANSWER 4:
An owner of a trademark applies to register his or her trademark by filing in the Patent and Trademark Office

(a) a written application,

(b) a drawing of the mark, and

(c) such number of specimens or facsimiles of the mark as used as may be required by the Commissioner.

Assignment B

ANSWER 1:
Inventor information, correspondence information, and application information.

ANSWER 2:
Walt Disney, 500 S. Buena Vista St., Burbank, California, 91521.

ANSWER 3:
No. Some of the marks that exist are
Way Cool Shred Now Work Later
Shredheds
The Shred Head
Incredibulls
The Incredible Clothing Company

ANSWER 4:
"Patents, Trademarks, and Copyrights," §2.25, p. 74.

CHAPTER 5

Employment/Labor Law

Assignment A

ANSWER 1:
5 U.S.C.A/U.S.C.S. §2302 deals with Government Organization and Employees; subpart A deals with General Provisions; and §2302 deals with Prohibited Personnel Practices. *Tucker v. Department of Health and Human Services*, 73 M.S.P.R. 278 (1997) held that an employee was not disqualified from seeking corrective action under the Whistleblower Protection Act, even though she had already sought redress by filing an action through the EEOC.

ANSWER 2:
Using the *BNA Fair Employment Practice Cases Cumulative Digest and Index*, 45-60 §108.4101 (Sex Discrimination), you will find *Hallquist v. Plumbers & Pipefitters*, Local 276, 47 F.E.P. Cases 3323 (1st Cir. 1988). The First Circuit held that the lower court properly held that the employer's stated reason for dismissal was a pretext. The employee showed that the employer intended to discharge its only woman and rearranged its male employees' vacation time in order to retain another male worker.

ANSWER 3:
Using the *Fair Employment Practice Cases*, §210.675, the answer is yes, according to *Hearn v. General Electric*, 71 F.E.P. Cases 435, (D. Ala. 1996), which held that an unlawfully laid-off female employee and an unlawfully demoted female employee were each entitled to an award of $75,000 in punitive damages against an employer whose plant manager acted with reckless indifference to their federally protected rights and who acted with malice in view of the evidence.

Assignment B

ANSWER 1:
For the definition of self-employed, see *Moriarty v. Svec*, 164 F.3d 323 (7th Cir. 1998), which defined a self-employed person as one who is not employed by another. *NLRB v. Drivers' Local Union No. 639*, 362 U.S. 274 (1960) held that Congress can prohibit self-employed persons from joining a union.

ANSWER 2:
An appropriate article is *The Big Lie: What Every Baby Boomer Should Know About Social Security and Medicare*, 5 J. of Pension Benefits 39-45, Autumn 1997. A pyramid scheme or Ponzi scheme uses money obtained by later investors to pay early investors.

ANSWER 3:
The National Labor Relations Act is comprehensive legislation regulating the relations between employers and employees; this act established the National Labor Relations Board. *Black's Law Dictionary*.

29 U.S.C., Chapter 7, Subchapter IV, is the appropriate code section for liabilities and restrictions on labor management.

A relevant treatise is *NLRB Practice, National Labor Relations Act: Law and Practice Procedure Before the National Labor Relations Board*, Washington, D.C., BNA, 1999, and another version by ALI-ABA.

CHAPTER 6

Securities

Assignment A

ANSWER 1:
The state of incorporation is Delaware. You can find an annual report at the local public library, or on Westlaw (through Dialog) using the database, SECAR and the search co(Microsoft). Dialog charges for the full text of annual reports. You can also find annual reports through Lexis on the library in a file called COMPNY;ARS. (Lexis does not charge.)

ANSWER 2:
The SIC Code is 7370. You can find a 10K at some local public libraries. You can also find the 10K using the Westlaw database SEC-10K. (Dialog charges for the full text of 10Ks). Lexis has 10Ks in the library and file—COMPNY;10Q.

ANSWER 3:
Some local public libraries have 1OQs. Westlaw has 10Qs on the database SEC-10Q. (Dialog charges for the full text.) Lexis has 10Qs on COMPNY;10Q. The auditors are Deloitte and Touche.

ANSWER 4:
Alan Palmiter's *Securities Regulation: Examples and Explanations* has an answer. A company goes public by selling its voting common shares for the first time to unrelated investors. The sale is made by means of a registration statement filed under the Securities Act. Once sold, the shares can be traded in a public trading market, such as the New York Stock Exchange or NASDAQ. In Microsoft's case, the shares were traded on the computer-based NASDAQ.

ANSWER 5:
5 Fed. Sec. L. Rep. ¶31,102 at 22,061 (1997) has a 10K form.

ANSWER 6:
15 U.S.C.A. §78(c)(51)(b)(1999) explains penny stock:

(51)(A)The term "penny stock" means any equity security other than a security that is

1. registered or approved for registration and traded on a national securities exchange that meets such criteria as the Commission shall prescribe by rule or regulation for purposes of this paragraph;
2. authorized for quotation on an automated quotation system sponsored by a registered securities association, if such system (I) was established and in operation before January 1, 1990, and (II) meets such criteria as the Commission shall prescribe by rule or regulation for purposes of this paragraph;
3. issued by an investment company registered under the Investment Company Act of 1940 [15 U.S.C.A. §80a - 1 et seq.];
4. excluded, on the basis of exceeding a minimum price, net tangible assets of the issuer, or other relevant criteria, from the definition of such term by rule or regulation which the Commission shall prescribe for purposes of this paragraph; or

5. exempted, in whole or part, conditionally or unconditionally, from the definition of such term by rule, regulation, or order prescribed by the Commission.

(B) The Commission may, by rule, regulation, or order, designate any equity security or class of equity securities described in clause (i) or (ii) of subparagraph (A) as within the meaning of the term "penny stock" if such security or class of securities is traded other than on a national securities exchange or through an automated quotation system described in clause (ii) of subparagraph (A).

Assignment B

ANSWER 1:
Robert Hamilton's *The Law of Corporations in a Nutshell* lists the elements:

> It shall be unlawful for any person, directly or indirectly, by the use of any means or instrumentality of interstate commerce, or of the mails or of any facility of any national securities exchange,
>
> 1. to employ any device, scheme, or artifice to defraud;
> 2. to make any untrue statement of a material fact or to omit to state a material fact necessary in order to make the statements made, in light of the circumstances under which they were made, not misleading; or
> 3. to engage in any act, practice, or course of business which operates or would operate as a fraud, or deceit upon any person, in connection with the purchase or sale of any security.

Relevant U.S. Supreme Court cases are *Santa Fe Industries, Inc. v. Green*, 430 U.S. 462 (1977) or *Ernst & Ernst v. Hochfelder*, 425 U.S. 185 (1976).

ANSWER 2:
Aaron v. SEC, 446 U.S. 680 (1980); *Ernst & Ernst v. Hochfelder*, 425 U.S. 185 (1976).
In Re Aetna, Inc., Fed. Sec. L. Rep. (CCH)—¶90,416 at 91,885 (1999).

ANSWER 3:
Thomas Lee Hazen, *The Law of Securities Regulation*, has the answer.

The Chinese Wall theory originated in the settlement of the *Matter of Merrill Lynch, Pierce, Fenner, and Smith, Inc.*, Securities Exchange Act Release No. 8459 (1967-69 Transfer Binder), Fed. Sec. L. Rep. (CCH) 1577,629 (1968). When *Merrill Lynch*, who was serving as the managing underwriter for an offering of Douglas Aircraft securities, passed on non-public information concerning an expected drop in earnings to favored *Merrill Lynch* customers, who in turn, sold their Douglas Aircraft holdings. After having initiated proceedings against *Merrill Lynch* and some of its employees, the SEC and *Merrill Lynch* entered a settlement order, accepting *Merrill Lynch's* new procedures for preventing dissemination of confidential non-public information by the underwriting department to other branches of the firm. While the SEC endorsed Merrill Lynch's new procedures, the SEC stated, "As a matter of Commission policy, we do not and indeed cannot, determine in advance that the statement of policy will prove adequate in all circumstances that may arise." The procedures implemented by Merrill Lynch, though not expressly named, have come to be known as Chinese walls.

ANSWER 4:
No. Uniform Securities Act T5541, §40(d) at 1563 (1997), Blue Sky Reporter, Chicago, Illinois, CCH (1999).

CHAPTER 7

International Law

Assignment A

ANSWER 1:
JX 236 1950 is the Call Number. The treaty is called Agricultural Commodities, March 20,1984, Item IV B, U.S. - Pakistan, Agreement, 1984; it was signed on March 20, 1984.

Limitations apply to soybean and cottonseed oil, sunflower oil, sesame oil, etc. *U.S. Treaties and Other International Agreements*, Washington, D.C., U.S. Department of State, 1950.

ANSWER 2:
Its citation in the Statutes at Large: 46 Stat. 2743.

Its date of signature: October 21, 1929.

Its number, for example, T.S. No. 668: T.S. No. 813.

Is it in force? Yes, as of February 15, 1993.

Treaty of Commerce and Navigation, April 22, 1930, U.S.–Turkey, 1930, *Treaties in Force: A List of Treaties and Other International Agreements of the U.S. in Force on January 1, 1994.*

ANSWER 3:
2 *Digest of Commercial Laws of the World:* Digest of Intellectual Property Laws (1991).
Two kinds of patents are invention and addition.

ANSWER 4:
Lexis library and file: INTLAW;UKCODE
Search protection w/3 trading w/3 interests w/3 act. It's number 87 of 58.

ANSWER 5:
Call the Embassy or Consulate of the Dominican Republic (in Miami) or in Washington, D.C.

Assignment B

ANSWER 1:
No, in Peru, the law does not make a distinction between civil and commercial contracts.
The Commercial Laws of Peru, Dr. Jose Ed. Clark, 5 *Digest of Commercial Laws of the World.*

ANSWER 2:
Dictionary of International and Comparative Law. Sharia is Islamic Law (Koranic Law).

ANSWER 3:
Westlaw
USTreaties (Database)
Search: Saudi Arabia & United States
Lexis
INTLAW (Library)
USTRTY (file)
Search: Saudi Arabia and United States and air transport
Air Transport Agreement Between the Government of the U.S.A. and the Government of the Kingdom of Saudi Arabia, entered into force on October 2, 1993, State Dept. No. 93-199 (Treaty).

CHAPTER 8

Medical Research

Assignment A

ANSWER 1:
The *Directory of Medical Specialists* contains the names of several specialists from Pittsburgh and is arranged geographically and by physician's name. Among others, in Pittsburgh, Dr. Toby O. Graham of Presbyterian University Hospital is Board Certified in Internal Medicine. His address is University of Pittsburgh, 200 Lothrop Street, Pittsburgh, PA 15213.

To find a definition of mesothelioma, use *Tabor's,* which describes mesothelioma as a rare malignant cancer of the pleura (membrane that lines the lungs). *Robbins* also describes mesothelioma as mesotheliomas being associated with asbestosis and that they were the cause of 5% of asbestosis cases.

Use Medline (Medline on Westlaw and Medlne;Medlne on Lexis, or http://medline.cos.com on the Internet) or the *Index Medicus* to find the article. Some ways of access are by the subject words: mesothelioma, etiology, or asbestos workers, asbestos-adverse effects. You could also do a search by title.

If you use Medline (Westlaw), search: malignant /3 mesothelioma /s asbestos /3 exposure. Lexis: malignant w/3 mesothelioma w/10 asbestos w/3 exposure. Other searches also work on Lexis and Westlaw. Medline has an accompanying thesaurus, which you could use to find your search terms, and then do the actual search.

Assignment B

ANSWER 1:
You can find a definition of Salk and Sabin vaccines in a medical dictionary. *Taber's* defines Salk vaccine as the first successful poliomyelitis vaccine; it contains three types of inactivated poliomyelitis viruses and induces immunity against the disease. *Taber's* defines Sabin vaccine as a live oral polio virus vaccine.

You can search in *Index Medicus* for an article to define and contrast the differences. Look under poliomyelitis or vaccine, Salk or Sabin.

You can also search on Medline. For example, on Westlaw through Dialog, search Medline: polio/3 vaccine /10 Salk Sabin. One of the articles describes Salk vaccine as an oral, live virus, discovered in 1960, which the patient could not recover on a breach of warranty claim, but material issues of fact existed, and a summary judgment claim was precluded. Salk vaccine is an inactive vaccine.

On Lexis, use Medlne/Medlne and search: polio w/10 Salk or Sabin w/10 vaccine.

An article is *A Calculated Risk: The Salk Vaccine Field Trials of 1954*, 317 B.M.J., No. 7167, 1233-6 (Oct. 31, 1998).

To find federal cases, use a federal digest such as West's *Federal Practice Digest,* 3rd or 4th, and search under negligence or pharmaceutical companies.

On Westlaw, search in Allfeds: pharmaceut! /p polio /p Salk /3 vaccine. You retrieve these cases, among others: *Snawder v. Cohen*, 749 F.Supp. 1473 (W.D. Kentucky, 1990) and *Staples v. Secretary, Dept. of Health and Human Services*, 30 Fed. Cl. 348 (1994), which held the National Childhood Vaccine Injury Act limited compensation for community acquired polio to those who received it from recipients of oral vaccine, and the patient could not recover on a breach of warranty claim, but material issues of fact existed, and a summary judgment claim was precluded. On Lexis, use Genfed, Courts, and search similarly: pharmaceut! W/10 polio w/10 Salk w/3 vaccine.

Assignment C

ANSWER 1:
See the picture in *Robbins*.

CHAPTER 9

Wills and Estates

Assignment A

ANSWER 1:
Page 7-519.

ANSWER 2:
Requirements for retirement benefits are found at ¶930, 032, of the *CCH Pension Plan Guide*. 4.1 discusses normal retirement: A participant shall be eligible for an early retirement pension if his employment is terminated on or after his 55th birthday and after he has completed 10 or more years of service.

ANSWER 3:
The Consolidated Omnibus Budget Reconciliation Act (COBRA) of 1985 allows certain individuals the right to continue health insurance coverage. Employees and their dependents who lose insurance coverage under the State health plan have the right to elect to continue coverage by paying the required premiums themselves. (Under COBRA, retirees and those covered through the "Direct Bill program" have the same continuation rights as active employees.)

Former employees, spouses, and dependents eligible to continue health insurance coverage are called Qualified Beneficiaries. The provisions under which they can continue coverage are called Qualifying Events. The number of months they can continue coverage is specified.

Health Coverage That Continues Under COBRA

Qualified beneficiaries are eligible to continue only those medical and dental benefits for which they are covered at the time of the qualifying event.

> NOTE: If an employee goes on Leave Without Pay (LWOP) and then terminates employment AND the employee does not continue Group Health Insurance coverage during the leave period, that employee and any dependents would not be eligible for COBRA continuation because they were not participating in the Group Health Insurance program at the time of the qualifying event.

A qualified beneficiary may elect to continue only health benefits. However, dental benefits can be continued only if health benefits are continued.

Employees may get information about continuing their coverage from the Employer Benefits Coordinator.

Duration of Coverage Continuation

Insurance coverage will continue for the number of months applicable to the qualifying event listed above unless one of the following occurs first:

1. Nonpayment or untimely payment of premiums;
2. The employee or their dependent(s) become(s) covered, either as an employee or dependent, under another employer-provided medical plan which does not limit or exclude coverage for pre-existing conditions (does not apply to the surviving spouse in qualifying event (C)).
3. The employee or enrolled dependent(s) become eligible for Medicare (has enrolled in the Medicare program). Only the person(s) eligible for Medicare coverage lose COBRA.

Continuation benefits. Any other person(s) enrolled may continue for the duration of the COBRA eligibility period.

Administration Issues

- Group health insurance benefits will terminate on the last day of the payroll period in which the qualifying event occurs.
- COBRA continuation is not automatic; it is a choice that the qualified beneficiary must make. The qualified beneficiary must complete the COBRA election form that accompanies the COBRA notification letter sent by the Benefits Coordinator. The qualified beneficiary has 60 days from the date of the letter to return the COBRA continuation election form to the Benefits Unit.
- COBRA notification letters will be sent to the qualified beneficiary at their last known address. Therefore, it is very important that a correct address appears on the Change Form or is correct in the payroll system at the time of termination. If the qualified beneficiary is a dependent, there should be a current address for the qualified beneficiary on the form. This is especially important when the qualifying event is divorce. Also, former employees should be reminded to leave forwarding instructions at the Post Office in the event of a change of address.

Benefit Costs—COBRA Continuation Rates

Any qualified beneficiary who elects to continue coverage under the plan must pay the full cost of that coverage (including both the share they paid as an active employee, and the share the employer paid).

ANSWER 4:
Yes. ¶15009, *CCH COBRA Guide*, IRS proposed regulation §1:162, Question and Answer A-18(c) says if coverage is dropped in contemplation of a qualifying event, the qualified beneficiary whose coverage is dropped will be just as much entitled to COBRA as if he or she had not been dropped.

ANSWER 5:
Page 1, Vol. 4, *Florida Probate Code*, pages 178-190 for model wills.

Assignment B

ANSWER 1:
Atkinson on Wills has the general requirements for testamentary capacity.

> To make a valid will one must be of sound mind, though he need not possess superior or even average mentality. One is of sound mind for testamentary purposes only when he can understand and carry in his mind in a general way:
>
> 1. The nature and extent of his property,
> 2. The persons who are the natural objects of his bounty, and
> 3. The disposition which he is making of his property.
>
> He must also be capable of:
>
> 4. Appreciating these elements in relation to each other, and
> 5. Forming an orderly desire as to the disposition of his property.

As shown above, testamentary capacity is determined according to one's mental ability to make a will; one may have testamentary capacity though he is under guardianship or lacks the ability to make a contract or transact other business.

Extreme old age does not disqualify one from making a will.

ANSWER 2:
Estate w/3 planning 2/3 form!

The basic formalities for drafting a durable power of attorney for property management are

1. the document should define the physical conditions under which the client wishes the health care agent to withhold or discontinue treatment;
2. the document should specify any types of medical procedures that the client wishes to forego or discontinue;
3. the document should describe under what circumstances the health care agent may give consent on the client's behalf; and
4. the document should describe the procedure used to determine that the client is unable to consent to treatment.

ANSWER 3:
Some relevant New York Estate Planning forms are
§7:548borc
§7:38
§3.279A

One of the appropriate forms is (as copied):
S3:279A

Order Vacating Probate Decree and Dismissing Probate of Will
On Basis of Lack of Testamentary Capacity [Form]
At a Surrogate's Court held in and for the County of ______________,
At ______________, on the _____ day of ____________, 19________.
Present: Hon. __________________, Surrogate,
[Add title of proceeding]
ORDER
File No. _______________

The Petitioner, _________________, having moved this court by way of order to show cause dated _________________, 19_______, for an order setting aside and vacating a previous decree of this court date ________________, 19___ which decree admitted to probate a document purporting to be the Last Will and Testament of the decedent, ________________, dated ____________, 19______, declaring that the said document was not the Last Will and Testament of the testator.

Signed ______________________________________

Dated _______________________________________

ANSWER 4:
Merrick v. Continental Illinois Bank, 10 Ill. App. 3d 104, 293 N.E.2d 767 (1973), held that beneficiaries under a will were necessary parties to the will contest. However, the beneficiaries should not have been defaulted for failure to appear or to file a responsive pleading. Even if an order of default had been entered in a will contest, it would have availed petitioner who contested the will nothing—since a default would not have afforded a proper basis for depriving those beneficiaries of their bequests if the will had been otherwise sustained as valid.

CHAPTER 10

Government Publications/Legislative Histories

Assignment A

ANSWER 1:
John E. Huerta is the General Counsel. His telephone number is (202) 357-1997.

This information is also available on the Internet on the Smithsonian Institution home page located at: http://www.si.edu/.

ANSWER 2:
This answer varies by state.

ANSWER 3:
Her address is 205 Congress House Office Building, Washington, D.C. 20515-0514. Her telephone number is (202) 225-8104. The state she represents is California.

This information is also available on the Thomas home page located at http://thomas.loc.gov/.

ANSWER 4:
7.74 HK$/1US$

This information is also located on the following Websites:
http://www.census.gov/statab/www
http://www.census.gov

ANSWER 5:
Number - 28; *U.S. Vital Statistics of the U.S.*

ANSWER 6:
Andrew M. Cuomo is the Secretary of Housing and Urban Development. His address is 451 7th St., SW, Washington, DC, 20410. His telephone number is (202) 708-1422. The 1998-99 edition was used and the information was located on page 300.

This information is also located on the Internet at the following Web address:
http://www.access.gpo.gov/nara/nara001.html

Assignment B

ANSWER 1:
The CIS number for the Federal Election Campaign Act Amendments is 77 S683-11, which is found in the CIS Cumulative Index 75-78, Vol. 6-9.

ANSWER 2:
The abstract is located in the *CIS* 1977 Abstracts, Vol. 8, No. 1-1 2, 1059.

ANSWER 3:
These amendments recommend passage of S.926, containing two provisions: Part 1, to provide for financing of Senatorial candidates from general revenue funds beginning in 1978, and Part 2, to amend the Federal Election Campaign Act of 1971, to reduce campaign recordkeeping

and recording requirements, and exempt certain political activities from act restrictions. CIS 1977 Abstracts, Vol. 8, No. 1-12, 1059.

ANSWER 4:
The Report Number is 95-300, at 1059 (1977) - CIS 1977 Abstracts, Vol. 8, No. 1-12,1059.

ANSWER 5:
The date of approval is June 24, 1977, and was found in CIS 1977 Abstracts, Vol. 8, No. 1-1 2, 1059.

ANSWER 6:
Part 2 reduces campaign recordkeeping and reporting requirements, and exempts certain political activities from act restrictions, as found in CIS 1977 Abstracts, Vol. 8, No. 1-12, 1059.

ANSWER 7:
Two of the principles are

- Principle 4, which establishes an overall expenditure limit for both general and primary elections; and
- Principle 5, which permits candidates to raise a limited amount of private funds in very small contributions.

The answers are found in Election Campaign Act, Pub. L. No. 93-443, 1974 *U.S.C.C.A.N.*, 93rd Congress 2d, Vol. 3, 5589.

ANSWER 8:
Yes, minor parties with significant support are eligible to receive a fair share of public assistance commensurate with their proven political strength. Election Campaign Act, Pub. L., No. 93-443, 1974 *U.S.C.C.A.N.*, 93rd Cong., 2d, Vol. 3, 5589.

ANSWER 9:
The resolution deals with granting copyright provisions to Inna Hecker Grade and her successors and assigns in the works set forth in section 2 by Chaim Grade for a term of 50 years from June 26, 1982. See the relief of Hecker Grade, H.R. 320,106th Cong., 1st Sess. (1999).

ANSWER 10:
The sponsor is Mr. Engel. (H.R. 320, 106th Cong., 1st Sess. 1999).

CHAPTER 11

Environmental Law

Assignment A

ANSWER 1:
Clean Air Act, 42 U.S.C. §7401–7671q. The amendments were passed in 1970 (P.L. 91-604),1977 (P.L. 95-95), and 1983 (P.L. 98-213).

ANSWER 2:
Environmental Law in a Nutshell explains the "bubble concept" as follows. The basic idea behind the "bubble concept" is to treat the various components of an industrial complex as a single source for regulatory purposes. Thus, emissions from all stacks are considered only in the aggregate. "Bubbles" involve multiplant facilities under common ownership.

ANSWER 3:
In *Chevron, U.S.A., Inc., v. N.R.D.C.*, 467 U.S. 837 (1984), the Supreme Court upheld the use of the bubble and the regulation allowing states to treat all pollution-emitting devices within the same industrial group as though they were encased in a single bubble. The Court found nothing in the language of the Clean Air Act or in the legislative history directly on point. The Supreme Court concluded that the issue was really one best decided by the EPA, rather than by the judiciary since judges were not experts in the field.

ANSWER 4:
120 days

ANSWER 5:
Yes. A "major statutory source" is any statutory facility or source of air pollutants which directly emits, or has the potential to emit, 100 tons or more of any air pollutant.

Assignment B

ANSWER 1:
Volume 8, *Treatise on Environmental Law*, "Primary Source Manual" states that the purpose of NEPA is as follows. NEPA is the basic national charter for the protection of the environment. It establishes policy, sets goals, and provide means for carrying out the policy. There are also "action forcing" provisions to make sure the federal agencies act according to the letter and spirit of the act. The purpose of these provisions is to tell federal agencies what they must do to comply with the procedures and to achieve the goals of the act. The President, the federal agencies, and the courts share responsibility for enforcing the act.

ANSWER 2:
Blue Mountains Biodiversity Project v. Blackwood

ANSWER 3:
Philip M. Ferester, *Revitalizing the NEPA: Substantive Law Adaptations from NEPA's Progeny*, 16 Harv. Envtl L. Rev. 207 (1992).

ANSWER 4:
20 E.L.R. 35219 (1989) is the cite. The time period is not less than 45 days.

ANSWER 5:
3–Environmental Reporter N.E.W.S. Waste Management

CHAPTER 12

Criminal Law/Criminal Procedure

Assignment A

ANSWER 1:
Kenny could be charged with Unlawful Possession of a Controlled Substance. Federal Criminal Code (1998), Title 21, U.S. Code, §841 and §844.

ANSWER 2:
Wharton's Criminal Law, Volume II, §107, page 47—intoxication involves an impairment of mental or physical capacity as a result of alcohol, drugs, or some other substance. Model Penal Code §2.08(a) Proposed Official Draft, 1962.

ANSWER 3:
Volume 64, *BNA Criminal Law Reporter*, Number 24, page 472. The case is *Foote v. Spiegel*, D. Utah, 2/23/99. This Americans with Disabilities Act was thrown out by the U.S. District Court for the District of Utah, and the suit against the officer was dismissed. The person had mild cerebral palsy, which affected her balance and coordination.

ANSWER 4:
Yes, *Wharton's Criminal Evidence*, page 614. The appropriate case is *Harrell v. U.S.*, 220 F.2d 516 (5th Cir. 1955).

ANSWER 5:
Bailey, *Investigation and Preparation of Criminal Cases*, §20.19. Yes.

ANSWER 6:
No. *Terry v. Ohio*, 392 U.S. 1 (1968), held that an illegal arrest or other unreasonable seizure of the person is itself a violation of the Fourth and Fourteenth Amendments. However, if there is reasonable cause to believe, the search is not unreasonable. *Terry* indicates that a two-step process must ordinarily be followed: the officer must pat down first, and then intrude beneath the surface of the suspect's clothing only if he comes upon something which feels like a weapon.

Assignment B

ANSWER 1:
Kenny can be charged with violation of Virginia Code 18.2-250. 1—possession of marijuana, and reckless driving 46.2-852. (Answer will vary).

ANSWER 2:
A definition of possession can be found in *Defending Drug Cases, and Model Jury Instructions*. To find the defendant guilty of possession, one must believe beyond a reasonable doubt that the defendant, with knowledge of its nature and character, intentionally and consciously exercised dominion and control over the item.

ANSWER 3:
The Virginia Code §18.2-266 states that it is unlawful to drive any motor vehicle while such person is under the influence of any narcotic drug or any other self-administered intoxicant of drug of whatsoever nature, or any combination of such drugs, to the degree which impairs his ability to drive or operate any motor vehicle. (Answer will vary.)

ANSWER 4:
Yes, *Wharton's Criminal Evidence*, p. 614. *Harrell v. U.S.*, 220 F.2d 516 (5th Cir. 1955).

ANSWER 5:
(Varies by state.) See *Foote v. Spiegel*, F.Supp. (D.Utah 1998), which held that the ADA did not protect a motorist who suffered from neurological problems when she was arrested when a state trooper mistakenly thought she was drug impaired.

ANSWER 6:
Ann can testify. See §20.19, non-expert testimony, F. Lee Bailey's *Investigation and Preparation of Criminal Cases*.

ANSWER 7:
Defending Criminal Cases in Virginia discusses probable cause: A search and seizure of private property may not be undertaken, except upon probable cause to believe that seizable objects are located at the place to be searched. In order to search a defendant before arresting him, the police must have reasonable suspicion that a crime has or will be committed. *Terry v. Ohio*, 392 U.S. 1 (1968).

CHAPTER 13

Westlaw

Assignment A

ANSWER 1:
Some appropriate searches are
    Red w/10 color or dye w/20 food
    red & dye /p food & color
    red +s color dye /sfood

In *Fleming v. Florida Citrus Exchange*, 358 U.S. 153 (1958), the U.S. Supreme Court held that a temporary legislative action [amendment of 21 U.S.C.A. §342(c)] did not make moot the issue of delisting Red No. 32. As such, the Supreme Court held that where there was no evidence that level of ingestion of particular red coal tar color involved in human consumption of oranges to which such color had been added was harmful, but there was proof that such color had a poisonous effect upon animals when taken in quantities as low as 0.01% of diet, the Secretary of Health, Education and Welfare properly removed the certification of such color as harmless and suitable for use as external coloring of oranges. *Fleming v. Florida Citrus Exch.*, 358 U.S. 153, (1958).

Certified Color Industry Comm. V. Secretary of Health, Education, and Welfare, 236 F.2d. 866 (2d Cir. 1956), was a case that tried to determine whether certain coal tar colors could be held as harmless. The Second Circuit held that in view of uncontradicted testimony showing that the least toxic of the three colors in question had a serious immediate effect on human beings, and that the overall effect on the laboratory animals, by proof on autopsy, was alarming. Evidence sustained a finding that addition of colors to food might render such food injurious to health, and the delisted colors were not harmless within the statute.

STATUTORY LAW

21 U.S.C.A. §301, Chapter 9 (1999)—Federal Food, Drug, and Cosmetic Act states, "the purpose of this chapter is to prevent other than harmless colors from being used in food, drugs and cosmetics."

Congress classified food as adulterated if added substances were injurious to health. The definition of "poisonous ingredient" was found in 21 U.S.C. 342(a)(1):

> If it bears or contains any poisonous or deleterious substance which may render it injurious to health; but in case the substance is not an added substance such food shall not be considered adulterated under this clause if the quantity of such substance in such food does not ordinarily render it injurious to health.

In response to the FDA's order, Congress amended 21 U.S.C.A. §342(c) on July 7, 1956, to require temporary certification of Red No. 32 until March 1, 1959.

In 1991, the FDA published its order for labeling of color additives: Congress amended 21 U.S.C. 376(c) to incorporate "coal tar dyes" among food colorings that required certification. Pursuant to the 1990 amendments to 21 U.S.C. 376 (c), the FDA amended 21 C.F.R. 101.22(k):

> The label of a food to which any coloring has been added shall declare the coloring in the statement of ingredients...manufacturers may parenthetically declare an appropriate alternative name of the certified color additive following its common or usual name.

The color industry developed Red No. 2, a substitute color for Red No. 32. It was less toxic, but still not certifiable under 21 U.S.C.A. §342(c). The statute would have to be further amended.

ADMINISTRATIVE REGULATIONS

21 C.F.R. §74.302(c)(1)(1998) states, "...shall be used only for coloring the skins of oranges that are not intended or used for processing...and that meet minimum maturity standards...."

Tests inconclusively indicated that certain coal tar colorings may have caused tumors in laboratory animals. On November 10, 1955, the Food and Drug Administration (FDA) ordered the removal of Red No. 32, a coal tar dye, from its list of food colorings that were harmless for human consumption since 1939.

The commissioner also terminated the provisional listing Red No. 2 for use in food in 21 *C.F.R. 81.10* in 1977.

LEGISLATIVE HISTORY

In 1959, the House's Committee on Interstate and Foreign Commerce published its rationale for the substitution of a color additive in H.R. Rep. 86-88: The committee was assured that the toxicity of Citrus Red No. 2 was significantly lower than Red No. 32. In fact, Red No. 2 was harmless to man in quantities necessary to color the skin of oranges. *U.S.C.C.A.N.* 1333 (1959).

LAW REVIEWS/JOURNAL ARTICLES

The *Food and Drug Law Journal* included two articles that debated the merits of labeling of carcinogens.

In her article, *Shoot First*, Marina Gatti, Esquire, questioned whether labeling would protect or confuse consumers:

> A requirement for warnings on all foods that may contain...a carcinogenic contaminant...would apply to many, perhaps all, foods in the supermarket. Such warnings would confuse the public, would not promote informed decision-making, and would not advance the public health. Warnings concerning deliberately added unbannable carcinogens do not present this difficulty. Marina Gatti, Esq., *Shoot First, Ask Questions Later*, 47 Food & Drug L.J. 739, 792 (1992).

In his article, *Reforming the Delaney Clause*, supra, Frederick Degnan, Esquire, questioned whether the FDA relaxed its standards for scientific evidence for a determination if a substance caused cancer. In fact, the FDA approved a large number of food additives not found to have induced cancer. However, these food additives were classified as carcinogens by organizations with less demanding standards. See Frederick Degnan, Esq., *Living with and Reforming the Delaney Clause*, 50 Food & Drug L.J. 235 (1995).

ALR

In his article for *American Law Reports*, Walter Jones Jr., Esquire, analyzed Fleming, supra, within his discussion of the principle of "harmlessness" of color additives. See Walter Jones Jr. Esq., *Validity, Construction, and Application of Color Additive Provisions of Federal Food, Drug, and Cosmetic Act*, 212 A.L.R. Fed. 475 (1972).

Therefore, Mrs. Brashford can bring a claim against the Florida Citrus Commission because the coloring has been found harmful in animal testing; and if she can prove that it was the cause of her rash, she can then prove the coloring harmful to her. It is obvious, according to the attached research, that the FDA is aware the coloring may be harmful.

Assignment B

ANSWER 1:
An appropriate search is TAMRA (Technical and Miscellaneous Revenue Act) and deduct ! /p obsolete

Use FTX-ALL "relevant entry" surfaced: 26 U.S.C.A. §168 (1999).

The U.S.C.A. database produced 26 U.S.C.A. §168 (1999).

TP-ALL indexed: Wendy Gerzog Shaller, *Limit Deductions for Mixed Personal/Business Expenses: Curb Current Abuses and Restore Some Progressivity Into the Tax Code*, 41 Cath. U.L. Rev. 581 (1992).

FTX-CS

Golden v. C.I.R. 58 T.C.M. (CCH) 185 (1989) held against the taxpayer.

Helstoski v. Commissioner 60 T.C.M. (CCH) 233 (1990) held against the taxpayer.

ALR and CFR produced no hits.

LH (Legislative History) indexed: H.R. Rep. No. 101-984 (1990).

CHAPTER 14

Lexis

Assignment A

ANSWER 1:
The results are the same as the Westlaw assignment, except that there were no hits in the News library or in the Legislative History library. Also, Lexis indexes the *Food and Drug Law Journal*, but coverage on the journal does not begin until 1994. Two law reviews that are available are Lars Noah and Richard A. Merrill, *Starting from Scratch?: Reinventing the Food Additive Approval Process*, 78 Boston University L. Rev. 329 (April 1998), and Lars Noah, *The FDA's New Policy on Guidelines: Having Your Cake and Eating It Too*, 47 Catholic University Law Rev. 113 (1997).

Assignment B

ANSWER 1:
An appropriate search for this is TAMRA (Technical and Miscellaneous Revenue Act) and deduction or deduct! w/20 obsole!

GENFED: U.S.C.S. produces 26 U.S.C.S. section 167(a) Depreciation. The general rule is that there shall be allowed as a deduction a reasonable allowance for the exhaustion, wear, and tear (including a reasonable allowance for obsolescence):
of property used in trade or business, or
of property held for the production of income.
26 U.S.C.S. §6702 and §6703 are also relevant.

GENFED:COURTS produced:

Hall v. Commissioner, 71 T.C.M. (CCH) 1869 (1996), allowed as a depreciation deduction a reasonable allowance for obsolescence of property used. Petitioner was not entitled to deductions for Schedule C (b)(2)(A) of the Technical and Miscellaneous Revenue Act of 1988.

Schwartz v. Commissioner, 68 T.C.M. (CCH) 63 (1994), allowed as a depreciation deduction a reasonable allowance for obsolescence of property used. Petitioner was not entitled to a deduction under Schedule C (b)(2)(A) of the Technical and Miscellaneous Revenue Act of 1988.

Golden v. Commissioner, 58 T.C.M. (CCH) 185 (1989), allowed as a depreciation deduction a reasonable allowance for obsolescence of property used: 1002(a)(24) of the Technical and Miscellaneous Revenue Act of 1988 and 1002(a)(29) of the Technical and Miscellaneous Revenue Act of 1988; but *Golden* failed to establish the depreciation deductions claimed represented a reasonable allowance for obsolescence of property used.

Using LAWREV;ALLREV, three articles state that there can be a deduction, particularly in favor of activities that require physical labor from the taxpayer and against those activities that require only an investment of capital. Depreciation of many intangibles is denied on the theory that intangibles have an unlimited, or indeterminable life. See:

Mona L. Hymel, Tax Policy and the Passive Loss Rules: Is Anybody Listening? 40 Ariz. L. Rev. 615 (Summer 1998).

Matthew J. Barrett, *Determining an Individual's Federal Income Tax Liability When the Tax Benefit Rule Applies: A Fifty-Year Checkup Brings a New Prescription for Calculating Gross, Adjusted Gross, and Taxable Incomes*, Brigham Young University Law, Rev. 1 (1994).

Wendy Gerzog Shaller, *Limit Deductions for Mix Personal/Business Expenses: Curb Current Abuses and Restore Some Progressivity Into the Tax Code*, 41 Cath. U.L. Rev. 581 (Spring 1992).

Allen Walburn, *Depreciation of Intangibles: An Area of the Tax Law in Need of Change*, 30 San Diego Law Rev. 453 (Spring, 1993).

ALR

An ALR was found by using the search TAMRA (Technical and Miscellaneous Revenue Act).

ANNOTATION

Validity, Construction, and Application of Provisions for Assessment and Review of Civil Penalty Against Taxpayer Who Files Frivolous Income Tax Return, 84 *A.L.R. Fed*. 433 (1998).

Deductions were generally not allowed.

CODES

CFR produced:

Subchapter A, Part 1—Income Taxes, Normal Taxes and Surtaxes, Computation of Taxable Income, Items Specifically Excluded from Gross Income, 1.132-8 Fringe benefit nondiscrimination rules, 26 *C.F.R.* §1.32-8 (1999).

26 *C.F.R.* 1.179-6 (1999), Chapter I, Subchapter A—Normal Taxes and Surtaxes, Computation of Taxable Income, Itemized Deductions for Individuals and Corporations.

Neither of these CFR sections authorized a deduction.

NEWS;CURNWS did not produce any relevant documents.

Nothing in LEGIS (Legislative Histories).

GENFED;TC (Tax Court) produced:

Helstoski v. Commissioner, 60 T.C.M. (CCH) 233 (1990) held petitioners were not entitled to any deductions.

Jeffery v. Commissioner, 59 T.C.M. (CCH) (1990) held no deductions were allowed.
In summary, our client may have a difficult time claiming a deduction.

CHAPTER 15

Internet

Assignment A

ANSWER 1:

a. The bill number is H.R. (House Resolution) 357.

b. The bill was introduced on January 19,1999.

c. The short title is "Violence Against Women Act of 1999." The bill was referred to the Subcommittee on Housing and Community Opportunity on January 19, 1999.

ANSWER 2:

a. *Intellectual Property Law* by Dratler

b. 1991

c. The call number is KF 2927.D73. The publisher is Law Journal Seminars Press in New York.

ANSWER 3:

a. The date of the decision is September 12, 1995.

b. Eleventh Circuit

c. The Eleventh Circuit affirmed the decision of the District Court.

Assignment B

ANSWER 1:

a. Pennsylvania is in the Third Circuit.
b. The Third Circuit is located in Philadelphia, Pennsylvania.

ANSWER 2:

a. G. Donald Gerlach
   Reed, Smith, Shaw, and McClay
   435 Sixth Avenue
   Philadelphia, Pennsylvania 15219
b. 1960
c. Harvard

ANSWER 3:

a. He was the target of a 1996 bomb attack; he lost 4 fingers and had massive injuries to his torso, right eye, and eardrums.
b. 60%